The SOVEREIGN GRACE of GOD

GREAT CHRISTIAN BOOKS
FROM REFORMATION PRESS
LINDENHURST, NEW YORK

JAMES R.WHITE

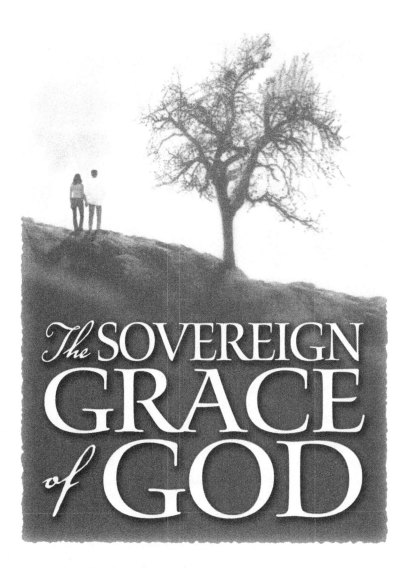

The SOVEREIGN GRACE of GOD

Great Christian Books / Reformation Press
160 37th Street
Lindenhurst, NY 11757
631. 956. 0998

ISBN: 978-0967084039

White, James R., 1963-
    The Sovereign Grace of God / James R. White
        p.   cm.
A "*A Great Christian Book*" book

Recommended Dewey Decimal Classification: 234
Suggested Subject Headings:
1. Religion—Christian literature—Apologetics.
2. Christianity—Calvinism—Grace.
3. The Bible—Theology—Doctrines of Grace.
4. The Bible—Doctrine—Salvation.
5. Theology—Soteriology—Calvinism.
I. Title

The book and cover design for this title are by Michael Rotolo.
It is typeset in the Minion family typeface by Adobe Inc. and is
quality manufactured on archival standard acid-free paper.
To discuss the publication of your Christian manuscript or
out-of-print book, please contact Reformation Press.

MANUFACTURED IN THE GREAT UNITED STATES OF AMERICA

About the Author

James White earned an M.A. from Fuller Theological Seminary, and the Th.M/Th.D from Columbia Evangelical Seminary. He serves as a Critical Consultant on the NASB Bible Update, as well as professor for Golden Gate Baptist Theological Seminary (Systematic Theology, Christology, Apologetics, Greek and Hebrew) and Columbia Evangelical Seminary. Dr. White is the Director of Alpha and Omega Ministries, a Christian Apologetics organization. He has authored over a dozen books defending God's sovereignty and grace, including: *Drawn By The Father, The Roman Catholic Controversy, and The Forgotten Trinity.* In addition to his writing he is also host of two regular radio programs, and as a veteran debater has engaged in over thirty moderated public debates against leading Roman Catholic apologists as well as numerous live radio debates with Latter Day Saints apologists. He is married to Kelli, and has two children, Joshua Daniel and Summer Marie.

Additional Books by the Author:

Drawn By The Father

The Roman Catholic Controversy

Mary— Another Redeemer?

Letters to A Mormon Elder

Is The Mormon My Brother?

The King James Only Controversy

What About The Dudes at The Door?

Grieving: Our Path Back to Peace

The Forgotten Trinity

To obtain any of the above titles or any
other Great Christian Books contact us at:
(631) 956-0998 or www.greatchristianbooks.com.
For group study ask for volume discounts!
*See also the other recommended titles
at the back of this book.*

Contents

Introduction

This book is for Christians— that is, for people who profess to believe in the Lord Jesus Christ and to trust Him for their eternal salvation. It is to believing, professing Christians that I am writing.

This book is for Christians who take the Bible seriously. I have a lot to say to those who reject the inspiration and authority of the Bible, and who replace that authority with their own concepts or their faith in "modern scholarship" (however that phrase is defined at the present time), but outside of a few comments in the first chapter, the text of this book is not the place for such a discussion. The fact that opposition to the inspiration and authority of the Bible often leads to a weak view of Scripture as well as serious errors in theology is dealt with in one of the appendices to this book.

I will not seek to defend the inspiration or accuracy of the Bible in this work. It must be a fact accepted as a presupposition to reading this book. If you believe that the Bible is both inspired and without error, and therefore authoritative, we have a solid foundation for this discussion of God's Sovereign Grace.

This book is for Christians who take the Bible seriously and who wish to believe only what is revealed in its pages. If you accept "other" Scriptures, or if you follow men or groups of men who claim a special "authority" of one kind or another that supposedly gives them the ability to announce the "only" proper interpretation of this Scripture or that, this book is not for you. I am not saying that you are not welcome to read it, I am just warning you ahead of time that I don't plan on taking any time to discuss how these issues relate to your position. I believe in *sola scriptura*— the Bible, and the Bible alone, is the *sole and sufficient* rule of faith for the Christian Church.

This book is *not* for the timid or the faint of heart. Unless you are already in complete agreement with me on the "doctrines of grace" as they are called, you will be challenged, and that without apology. I am not going to attempt to smother you under loads and loads of esoteric scholarly terms (although in the places where such is necessary it's been provided in footnotes or in an appendix). This is meant to be a friendly book, so if you ever start reading into it a nasty or joyless sort of voice, please realize that you are misreading me and my intentions. I say this because I've met folks that come across that way who call themselves Calvinists, but I think that anyone who *truly understands* what this is all about is going to be neither nasty nor joyless. My desire is to speak with you as I speak with any other person who shares with me a common commitment to Jesus Christ. But as the writer of the Proverbs said, iron sharpens iron, and when two believers sit down to discuss God's truth, some sharpening is (hopefully) going to take place.

This book is about the gospel of Jesus Christ. Yes, the subtitle reads *A Biblical Study of the Doctrines of Calvinism*, but that does not change the fact that this book is about the gospel. The issues that are involved in such an examination of Calvinism are simply the issues of the gospel— the role of God, the work of Christ, the need of man. While it may make it a little easier for us to avoid making the difficult decisions that this topic *forces upon us,* the fact remains that classifying the ancient *Calvinist/ Arminian* or *Pelagian/Augustinian* debate as a "non-essential" just doesn't make any sense. Whether God is sovereign in actually accomplishing salvation is hardly something that can be called "unimportant." Whether the work of Christ *actually accomplishes* redemption or *simply makes it a possibility* is not an issue that can be ignored. These things are vital to our understanding of the gospel itself, and a Church that has not struggled and wrestled with these issues is not going to be a Church that communicates the gospel to the lost with any semblance of clarity or accuracy.

I am quite aware of the *discomfort* that this topic can cause a believer. For some of us, being faced with the absolute sovereignty of God, recognizing that *whatever happens in this world* is part of His plan and is under His control, causes pain and discomfort. Believe me, if there was some way of sparing people any trauma in coming to grips with the true, Biblical God, I would follow that path. But I do not believe such a path exists. In fact, the reactions of men as they encountered the true God in Scripture invariably show us that such is a tremendously shaking experience. Isaiah the prophet, upon seeing God as He really is, confessed that he was "undone." How much more can we expect to be "undone" by facing, honestly and openly, the magnificent God whom we claim to worship?

It would be a denial of what I believe about the necessity of God's revealing these things to an individual to insist that all Christians immediately come into full and completely agreement with me on the doctrines of grace. I am not the Spirit of God, and I cannot *force* anyone to believe these things. The Bible teaches them, and I can simply trust God to lead His people into the truth about Him and His ways.

The format of this work is fairly straightforward. First, this is not an exhaustive work by any stretch of the imagination. It is my desire to explain the doctrines of grace as they are found in the Bible. I will not attempt to go over *every* Scripture that teaches such and such a truth. There are wonderful works that do that*, and there is no need to reinvent the wheel in that area. I have, in fact, done my level best to be succinct in my presentation, and to limit my selection of Scripture verses to a manageable number, so that the reader can have his or her Bible open and take the time to examine the texts in their proper setting and context without turning the reading of this book into a tremendously long affair. Furthermore, I wish to assure the reader that I am well aware of a wide variety of objections that are lodged against the presentation of the gospel that I am putting forward. In no way do I claim to even attempt to answer all the charges that are made against my position. You are again directed to other much larger (and, sometimes, less readable) works for further information on those subjects.

One objection that has often been lodged against Calvinists is that we are too "logical" in our study and presentation. You will note that the doctrines of grace are completely inter-connected, and they flow naturally from one to the next. But we believe that this is not the result of a foreign system of belief being forced upon the text of Scripture. Rather, because we believe in the full inspiration and inerrancy of the Bible, we believe that the consistency and harmony of the revelation of God results in the consistency and logic of the doctrines of grace that come forth from an honest examination of the text.

The only proper attitude for this discussion is one that is based upon, molded by, and directed toward, a sincere, deep

---

*Obtain some of the following works: Louis Berkhof, *Systematic Theology*, (Grand Rapids, Win. B. Eerdman's Publishing Co., 1941, 4th ed.), Charles Hodge, *Systematic Theology*, (Grand Rapids: Win. B. Eerdman's Publishing Co., 1986, or John Calvin, *Institutes of the Christian Religion*, (Philad.: Westminster Press, 1960). All are available through the Great Christian Books bookstore from Reformation Press, see page 199 of this book for other recommended titles and how to contact us.

desire to know the truth of God, no matter what that means. If you are looking to find a comfortable view of the gospel that does not offend the lost and asks nothing from the Christian, you won't find it here! But if you desire to really know what the Bible teaches, then set aside a couple of hours, get comfortable, make sure your Bible is close at hand, and don't forget a notepad for the inevitable questions that will come up— *Now let's look to the Word of God!*

1

The Basis of Inquiry: The Word of God

Therefore let God-inspired Scripture decide between us; and on whichever side be found doctrines in harmony with the word of God, in favour of that side will be cast the vote of truth. — *Basil of Caesarea*

Experience has taught me that it is best to start at the beginning and work up from there. One must have a solid foundation upon which to build, or problems will be inevitable. So it is with discussing the nature of the gospel of Jesus Christ, and how such issues as predestination and election are related to what God has done in Christ.

It would seem superfluous to say that the Bible as God's Word must be our final court of appeal, but it needs to be said anyway. The issues with which we are dealing are intensely personal in nature, and many people will be called to radically alter their view of God, themselves, and the world in the process of an honest examination of the issues that make up the subject of this book. What this means is that people who otherwise would never think of questioning the truth of the Bible have more than once, upon being faced with the fact of God's absolute sovereignty and election of some (but not all) unto salvation, in a fit of emotionalism, have retorted, "If that is what God is like, I want nothing to do with Him!" They could not, in their agitated state, see that they were making their own likes and desires the final court of appeal, the final source of authority. They were showing that all of us, to some degree, "selectively edit" what we want to believe from the Bible, and the rest is simply ignored or, even worse, rejected. We need to be reminded that we are sinful beings, with imperfect minds and perceptions, and this is why we must be totally submitted to the authority of Scripture in all things.

Surely it is obvious that the entire discussion of the doctrines of grace is a superfluous one for those who do not accept the inspiration and authority of the Bible. Sadly, we must admit that this means that a large portion of modern "Christendom" will have no common basis upon which we can discuss this topic. If one does not believe that the Bible is "God-breathed" one will not put a tremendous amount of effort into an attempt to determine the consistent testimony from the Bible on predestination and election simply because no such consistency is believed to exist! For those who feel that the Bible presents many different teachings and is contradictory to itself, our exercise here will be a classic example of wasting paper and ink. History teaches us that it is a fact of life that simply because one generation has the truth and is willing to be committed to it does not mean that following generations will do so. It is glowing testimony to this reality that some of the modern denominations who once believed and taught God's sovereign grace today not only do not believe this, but do not believe in the Bible as the inspired Word of God any longer, either. God has never promised his blessings to remain upon a church that walks away from His truth.

But there are many, many today who strongly believe in the inspiration of Scripture but do not believe in the doctrines of grace. Why is this? There are a number of reasons. It might be helpful to look at a few.

First, many today have a "New Testament only" view of the Bible. Of course, we will see that the New Testament teaches predestination and election in no uncertain terms. But the view of

God that underlies these truths that of the sovereign Creator who disposes men and nations as He sees fit is provided to us primarily in the Old Testament. God revealed these basic truths about Himself first to the people of Israel. Unfortunately, many today find the Old Testament to be a closed book. Aside from a familiarity with some of the stories regarding creation, or a basic knowledge of such famous persons as Abraham or Moses, most modern Christians find little reason to spend much time attempting to understand the prophecies of Isaiah or Jeremiah, much less struggling with the issues raised by Habakkuk or Zephaniah. And if we wander into the history of Israel in 2 Kings we certainly feel out of place! We would certainly feel more at home in the third chapter of John!

The result of this kind of thinking is a view of the Bible that effectively removes two thirds of God's revelation from our understanding of the gospel of Christ. What is worse than this is the fact that many feel that we should avoid dealing with the difficult passages of the Old Testament, and should stick to "talking about Jesus." The Apostles, on the other hand, were immersed in the Old Testament, and did not feel that such study in any way detracted from proclaiming the truth of the Messiah. We cannot forget that 2 Kings is just as *inspired* as John 3, and God has a purpose in revealing all that He has revealed in Scripture. We may have "favorite" passages, but that does not mean that those passages are any more important than any others.

There is also a movement in our world today that decries the importance of doctrine or teaching. In an effort to bring about a surface-level unity, many who believe the Bible to be the Word of God compromise that very truth by denying that sound doctrine, based upon clear Biblical teaching, is necessary for real unity to exist. Instead, a higher authority has been accepted in the form of a nebulous concept of "unity." Those who would be so "narrow minded" as to discuss such issues as the doctrines of grace are seen as unloving dogmatists who have really missed the "true essence" of Christianity.

Others have bought into various forms of mysticism. This has resulted in a view of the Bible and the Christian faith that is based upon subjective feelings and experiences. For many, a logical, consistent interpretation of Scripture should not even be sought! Christian truth is not supposed to consistent, we are told, and to seek for such consistency is to force a foreign concept (that truth exists and God has revealed it in Scripture) upon the Bible. It is common for such folks to speak of the "tensions" in the Bible, which is a rather polite way to refer to contradictions, possibly not in the text, but certainly in the teaching, of Scripture. Some who fall into this category go so far as to delight in the concept of paradox, even when there is no real reason to do so!

But I do not want to keep the reader from getting to the subject of the work with preliminary discussions. Let me conclude this chapter by asserting the following: I ask you, as a fellow believer in Jesus Christ, to make a commitment, right now, to be an obedient child of God, and to listen to the words of the Holy Spirit that are given to us in Scripture. If you have any higher priority than being in line with the truth of God as found in the Word of God, set this book aside and pray that God will place in your heart (as only He can) a burning desire to know Him as He truly is, and to know the truth about the gospel. If this means laying aside long-held and cherished beliefs, then you must be willing to do this. We all must recognize that we need to be constantly reformed by the Word of God. None of us has a corner on truth. But thanks be to God that He has given us His unchanging Word, so that when we wander off into the trackless wastes of our own understanding, He can call us back to the standard of truth found in Holy Scripture. As we examine the doctrines of grace, let Isaiah's words be our motto:

> *To the law and to the testimony!*
> *If they do not speak according to this word,*
> *they have no light of dawn.*   — *Isaiah 8:20*

2

A Six-Pedaled Tulip:
The All-Important Starting Point

But the expression implies that it is God's mere will and sovereign pleasure, which supremely orders this affair. It is the divine will without restraint, or constraint, or obligation... The sovereignty of God in his absolute, independent right of disposing of all creatures according to his own pleasure. — *Jonathan Edwards*

Many discussions of theology, especially if they involve people with differing views, get absolutely nowhere for the simple reason that many today do not approach such discussions in the proper way. We often ignore the foundations of the argument, the most basic issues, and immediately jump to points way down the line. You have to find the starting point, the initial point of divergence in the argument, if anything is going to be accomplished. We must start at the beginning!

The classical expression of the Reformed understanding of the gospel has been summed up, for better or for worse, in the "Five Points of Calvinism." These five points were formulated by the Council of Dort (1618-1619) in response to the opposite position presented by a group of men known as the Remonstrants. Since the Five Points came out of the arena of conflict, they are hardly a comprehensive, exhaustive accounting of the Reformed doctrine of salvation. But, they do function to define what the Calvinist does, and does not, believe scripture teaches. The Five Points have been summed up in the little acrostic— "TULIP," which stands for:

$$T = \textit{Total Depravity}$$
$$U = \textit{Unconditional Election}$$
$$L = \textit{Limited Atonement}$$
$$I = \textit{Irresistible Grace}$$
$$P = \textit{Perseverance of the Saints}$$

Some prefer somewhat different names for each of the points, resulting in a dismantling of the acrostic, and as we address each point we will note alternative designations.

When the Five Points were originally formulated by the Council of Dort, those in attendance did not believe that they were creating some "new" doctrine by their definitions. Obviously, they believed that they were simply defining, against a *new error*, the gospel of grace always found in the New Testament. Our examination of the Scriptures, we believe, will show this to be the case. But when these ancient doctrines were first presented as the Five Points, there was one, large and looming "belief," a belief that is really the starting point of the entire system, that was left unexpressed, only because it was taken, at least formally, as a "given" at the time. Today, such a "given" cannot be assumed. So, we must start at the beginning, and present a "six-pedaled tulip."

At the root, the foundation, of the entire gospel of Christ as presented in the Bible, is one over-riding belief: God is sovereign ruler over all the universe. The "sovereignty of God" is surely a "buzz-word" with Calvinists, and we often are not clear in defining exactly what we mean by it. But, without a full and complete understanding of this vital truth, we will never have a solid foundation for understanding what comes later. I realize that adding the sovereignty of God as the "sixth" point to the scheme results in a "STULIP," but that doesn't matter. I've seen many a person, upon being confronted with the truth about the sovereignty of God, radically changed and altered by the Spirit of God (who had to open their eyes to see the true God in the first place). So, even if our acrostic is made somewhat less smooth by the insertion of the primary starting point, the necessity is there all the same.

Why has it become necessary to start with what is in fact one of the most basic elements of the knowledge of God? Why have so many people grown up within "Christian" churches, and yet do not even understand some of the most elemental truths about God? Much of it has to do with how we proclaim the gospel today. Our first introduction to the faith is through the proclamation of the gospel message to us. How often is God's sovereignty a part of that message? Sadly, hardly ever at all within modern evangelicalism. God is not presented as the King, the Sovereign Ruler of all things. He is presented as someone who would like to save men, if only they would allow Him to! When we are told that we are the ones who decide if God's entire effort on our behalf (including the death of His Son!) is going to be fruitful, or in vain, we automatically produce a picture of God that is far removed from the truth of Scripture.

So we must start with the truth about God before we can know the truth of what God has done to save us. We must know our God before we can fully appreciate His works. (Note: this topic, above all others, requires us to examine many passages of Scripture. It is absolutely necessary that each of the passages be read in its entirety, very carefully.)

The Uniqueness of God

"To whom will you compare me?
Or who is my equal?" says the Holy One.
Lift up your eyes and look to the heavens:
Who created all these?
He who brings out the starry host

one by one,
and calls them each by name.
Because of his great power and
mighty strength,
not one of them is missing.   —*Isaiah 40:25-26*

Uniqueness; One of a kind; Like no other. What does this mean when we apply the term to God? We know, of course, that there is only one God. This is the most basic revelation of God in all of the Bible. God is God, and nothing else is God. God created all else, so, by definition, everything else cannot be God! But are we simply affirming monotheism, the belief in one God, when we speak of God's uniqueness?

While it is true that there is only one God, His uniqueness speaks to more than just this. God is unique in that He is totally "other" than His creation. His nature is completely different than ours, or any other created being's. Therefore, any analogy or example that we might use will break down at some point. We simply can't compare God to anything, because to do so assumes that there can be anything in creation that can be likened to God. "To whom will you compare me?" God asks. No answer is given, for there simply is no answer. God cannot be compared to anyone or anything, for He is unique, alone as the Creator of all things. Isaiah challenged us to look up at the dark, night sky, and observe with wonder the stars of the heavens. Then, he tells us that our God is the one who brings out the starry host one by one and who guides their paths through the heavens. How can one begin to make comparisons with such a one as this?

No one is like you, O LORD; you are great, and your name
is mighty in power. Who should not revere you,
O King of the nations? This is your due. Among all the wise
men of the nations and in all their kingdoms,
there is no one like you.   — *Jeremiah 10:6-7*

"No one is like you...there is no one like you." Statements of uniqueness, this time from Jeremiah. God's uniqueness results in men owing him reverence and worship. His great power calls all men to bow down in worship before Him. Were it not for sin, this would be the "natural" response of the human heart. God is to be praised simply because He is God. That the great Jehovah would have dealings with men is an amazing thing. This is a predominant theme in the Psalter as well. Note the 113th Psalm:

> *Who is like the LORD our God, the One who sits enthroned on high, who stoops down to look on the heavens and the earth?* —Psalm 113:5-6

The unanswerable question of "who is like the LORD" is followed with the picture of God "stooping down" to look not just upon the earth, but upon the heavens as well! Like a man might stoop down to look at a small creature crawling upon the ground, so God looks down upon all creation itself! Is your heart filled with awe at such a God? Can you read the following lines from Isaiah without bowing in adoration and praise?

> *Who has measured the waters in the hollow of his hand, or with the breadth of his hand marked off the heavens? Who has held the dust of the earth in a basket, or weighed the mountains on the scales and the hills in a balance? Who has understood the mind of the LORD, or instructed him as his counselor? Whom did the LORD consult to enlighten him, and who taught him the right way? Who was it that taught him knowledge or showed him the path of understanding? Surely the nations are like a drop in a bucket; they are regarded as dust on the scales; he weighs the islands as though they were fine dust. Lebanon is not sufficient for altar fires, nor its animals enough for burnt offerings. Before him all the nations are as nothing; they are regarded by him as worthless and less than nothing. To whom, then, will you compare God?* — Isaiah 40:12-18

Who indeed has instructed God? Who has taught Him anything at all? When we address later issues, we will have occasion to note this passage again. We cannot compare God to anyone or anything. He is beyond our capacity to even describe, let alone fully comprehend.

Why is this important in a discussion of the gospel? Quite simply, it is our nature, as sinful rebels against God, to "re-create" Him in our own image. We place upon God human characteristics and motivations. But God denies that He is a man, or like creatures in His knowledge, power or purposes. We are uncomfortable with such a God. We want Him to be more like us, more susceptible to our failures, our problems.[1] His uniqueness should keep us from compromising the truth of God for the sake of presenting God in a (supposedly) less "threatening" way. We should seek God's truth about Himself and be content with that, if we are truly committed to the authority of His Word.

Living in Eternity

For this is what the high and lofty One says he who lives forever, whose name is holy: "I live in a high and holy place, but also with him who is contrite and lowly in spirit, to revive the spirit of the lowly and to revive the heart of the contrite." —Isaiah 57:15

Surely one of the most difficult things for us to understand about God is His *eternal nature*. We are limited to time we experience reality as a series of events— past, present and future. Our language is based upon our experience of time. We have past tenses, and present tenses, and future tenses. We think in a temporal, time-based way.

But God does not exist as we do. We have seen that He is unique, and one of the greatest ways in which this is seen is His relationship with time itself. When we speak of God as eternal, what do we mean? Are we simply asserting that God has always existed and will always exist? While that may be true, God's eternal nature is not limited to simply exhaustive existence for a very long, long time. We are speaking of God's actually *transcending* the boundaries of time, of existing outside of the realm of time! This is very important, so we must dig in and think this through.

> Do you not know? Have you not heard? The LORD is the
> everlasting God, the Creator of the ends of the earth.
> — Isaiah 40:28

Jehovah is the eternal, everlasting God. Yet, if He is limited to an existence within time, then we have to believe that time itself existed *prior* to God.[2] Is time an absolute that is higher than God? Is God subservient to time? Does time exist outside of God, beyond His control, and is He limited to it? Or is time itself a creation of God, defined and directed by Him? I believe the Bible clearly teaches the latter position, despite the difficulty we have in understanding it! God is the creator of all things, including time itself, and is therefore not bound to an existence that is marked by the "past— present— future" mode of being. There are a number of reasons why I believe this way, and more of them shall become evident as we examine the teaching of the Bible. For now, let us consider this passage from Isaiah:

> "Who has done this and carried it through, calling forth the
> generations from the beginning? I, the LORD— with the
> first of them and with the last— I am he."   —Isaiah 41:4

Listen to God's words carefully. Just as God "brings forth" the starry host and "calls them by name" in Isaiah 40:26, here He is described as the one who is "calling forth" the generations from the beginning. This is creation language, but here in reference to the "generations." He is "with" the first and the last of these generations.[3] He is not limited to these generations, but is their Creator, the one who orders them, and determines what will come about in them (see 41:2-3 for the context).

> Before the mountains were born or you brought forth
> the earth and the world, from everlasting to everlasting
> you are God.   —Psalm 90:2

God's existence as God cannot be defined by time terms.

What does it mean to exist "before" creation when time is something that is measured by change in the creation itself? God's timeless existence can be graphically represented in this way:

The line represents time itself, moving from left to right. As a created thing, it has a beginning, and it has an end. Along the line we have three events. The first is represented by the fire, this is Moses' encounter with God recorded in Exodus 3:14. Here God told Moses:

> *"God said to Moses, 'I AM WHO I AM'. This is what you*
> *are to say to the Israelites: 'I AM has sent me to you.' "*

God is the I AM, not simply the I WAS or the I HOPE TO BE. He is the eternal one.

The cross represents the focal point in history, the death of Jesus Christ at Calvary. The arrow toward the end of the line (which is not meant to indicate anything more than to provide a reference to where we may be along that line) represents our current stage in history.

Now imagine, if you will, that the entire oval represents the being of God. He surrounds the entire timeline. His being is "present" at each and every point along the line, and that equally. This is what we are talking about when we speak of God dwelling in eternity, or transcending time itself. He is not limited by it, but it is limited by Him.

A small amount of reflection on this concept will also reveal another aspect of this truth to us. If God does indeed exist in this way, then it follows that *all points in time are instantaneous to God*. That is, if God is not experiencing, as a necessity, a progression of events, then all points in time are "now" to God. He is constantly the I AM, because there is no past or future to the being of God.

What this means is, quite obviously, mind-boggling for us creatures. God has never once predicted the future. What I mean by this is that God does not simply sit here in the present with us and, through some strange power, peer into the future so as to be able to predict future events with uncanny accuracy. No, God does not "look into the future" because *He is already there!* He is *with* the first and the last of the generations as Creator, and all that takes place in time does so at His sovereign command, as we shall see at a later point. God's knowledge of the future, then, is based not upon predictive powers, but upon the simple fact that God created time, and is already present in that future that exists solely because He decreed it to be so.

It is often alleged that the Reformed insistence upon the eternality of God is derived from Greek philosophical influences. However, we find that the basis of our belief has been found in God's revelation in the Old Testament, not in Aristotle! This is part of God's basic, foundational revelation of His being. We shall see that this concept will come up again and again as we discuss other aspects of God's being. It will become even more clear how important it is that we accept this truth from the Word of God.

Immutability: Unchanging Perfection

In the beginning you laid the foundations of the earth, and the heavens are the work of your hands. They will perish, but you remain; they will all wear out like a garment, Like clothing you will change them and they will be discarded. But you remain the same, and your years will never end.
—Psalm 102:25-27

God does not change. He is not one thing today, and another tomorrow. He is *immutable*, that is, not susceptible to change or alteration. He remains the same, and His years will never end, simply because He is not subject to change and aging as His creation is. As James said, God "does not change like shifting shadows" (James 1:17).

We can see how this truth is related to what has come before. Change involves time. For something to change, it has to be one way at time X, and then change to something else at time Y. This is change. But since God is not limited to the progression of time, but exists in eternity, then how can He change? How can He be one thing at one point in time, and something else at another point in time, if all points in time are instantaneous to Him? God's immutability is closely connected with His eternal nature. Take away His immutability, and you have a limited, finite deity who is not only subject to time, but of necessity He becomes subject to change.

God is perfect and complete. He is "most Holy," which includes as a necessity perfection and completeness. God is lacking nothing. Yet, if God could change, we could no longer speak of His perfection and completeness. If something, or someone, is perfect, and then undergoes change, what is the result? Can perfection become "more perfect"? No, if perfection changes, it becomes imperfection. If that which is complete changes, it becomes incomplete. So, if God, who is perfect and complete, changes, then He must of necessity become imperfect and incomplete.

The only other option is that God is not perfect and complete to begin with, and is in a process of change so as to become perfect and complete. Sadly, this concept has many proponents today.[4] But the simplest response to such a presentation of God is this: such a god bears little, if any, resemblance to the God of the Scriptures.

We have difficulty "relating to" an unchangeable being. We change day by day, moment by moment. If man is anything, he is changeable! Our emotions can go from high to low in a matter of seconds, and along with them goes our entire view of the world. But God is not that way. He does not change, and is not constantly on a roller-coaster ride of emotions and desires. Some say this concept of God is "cold" and heartless. They prefer presentations of the deity that allow God to be understood in ways that seriously compromise and openly deny His immutability. And, in fact, are there not many passages of Scripture that speak of God in ways compatible with this perspective? Do we not read of God's displaying emotion and therefore change?

We do read such things in the Holy Scriptures. But we must differentiate between the means by which God has revealed Himself in Scripture, and the direct teachings of the Scriptures when they speak of how God exists. That is, we should be careful not to take the means God uses to tell us about Himself and understand them to be contradictory to the direct teachings of the Bible about God's eternality and immutability.

God has spoken to us in human language and human terms. Simply communicating with us is a great action of condescension on His part. One has written:

> "For who even of slight intelligence does not understand that, as nurses commonly do with infants, God is wont in a measure to "lisp" in speaking to us? Thus such forms of speaking do not so much express clearly what God is like as accommodate the knowledge of him to our slight capacity. To do this he must descend far beneath his loftiness.[5]

And with specific reference to this topic, our writer later said:

> "Surely its meaning is like that of all other modes of speaking that describe God for us in human terms. For because our weakness does not attain to his exalted state, the description of him that is given to us must be accommodated to our capacity so that we may understand it. Now the mode of accommodation is for him to represent himself to us not as he is in himself, but as he seems to us.[6]

The representations we have of God in Scripture, then, must be couched in language that is understandable to us. To even express God's truth in human language is going to result in difficulties, for our language can hardly speak of God's eternal nature, let alone give proper expression to it! What we see of God, then, is but the perspective of one looking up at something which is at a vast height above him. We see but one side of the object, and much is hidden from our sight. We would do well, then, to refrain from making rash judgments concerning the entirety of the object until further information is given to us.

To apply this example to our present discussion, we are told that God is eternal, and that He is the Creator of all things. We shall see below that God directly claims control over, and responsibility for, all actions that take place in time, and this further supports our belief that God is the Creator of time itself. Since we have this direct information, we should refrain from taking God's "lisping" in His revelation of Himself as if He experiences time like we do and using this to overthrow the clear witness of Scripture. We must not take our inferences, drawn as they are from our own experiences, and create out of them doctrines that are contrary to the clear teaching of God in the Word. Further, we must remember that it is sinful to desire to make God something that He is not. We, as sinful beings, will do all we can to avoid truly facing the holy God. With this in mind, we should examine our motivations for seeking a less than Biblical understanding of the nature of God.

The Maker, and Shaper, of Clay

To the LORD your God belong the heavens, even the highest heavens, the earth and everything in it.
—Deuteronomy 10:14

Israel, from her very beginning, confessed something that was tremendously revolutionary in that ancient day. Rather than a god who was limited to national boundaries, Israel confessed the God who had power over all nations. Rather than a deity who was a bit player in a large drama of creation involving many deities of higher or lower rank, Israel confessed that Yahweh had created the heavens and the earth. One God, Creator of all things.

The idea that God is Creator is basic to Jewish and Christian belief. God, the personal God who has revealed Himself in His creation, and in His Word, created, for a purpose, everything that exists in the universe. No matter what definition one uses— even if one postulates universe upon universe— God is the Creator still. Nothing exists outside of His desire to make it exist— nothing.

God did not have to create. He is not limited by, nor dependent upon, His creation. Unlike all the pantheists running about worshipping trees and rocks and insects, the Christian sees the creation as separate from God in the sense that God is not creation and creation is not God. There was a time (though such a term is not exactly accurate) when there was nothing but God. God, before creation, was perfect and complete and whole. But He decided, in His own will, to create. He created the universe for a purpose.

Everything that exists continues to do so because God wills it to be so. His power is so great that He controls the "electron cloud" around each atom in your body. Each time one molecule binds to another, He is there. His power is at work. In the infinitely small sub-atomic particle, and in the giant star, He is at work. His power sustains and upholds all that exists.

> The heavens are yours, and yours also the earth; you
> founded the world and all that is in it.   —Psalm 89:11

Every breath that you take is given to you as a gift of God. Every beat of your heart is possible only because He allows it. Every wondrous sight that enters your eye, every beautiful sound, is yours as a gift from His hand.

> This is what God the LORD says— he who created the
> heavens and stretched them out, who spread out the earth
> and all that comes out of it, who gives breath to its people,
> and life to those who walk on it.   —Isaiah 42:5

This is the God who takes a tiny cell and turns it into a smiling, happy child. This is the God whose hands formed you in the womb and made you what you are today (Psalm 139:13-16). God needed no help in creation. "He spoke, and it came to be; he commanded, and it stood firm" (Psalm 33:9). He relied upon no outside help, nor did He derive assistance from some other deity.

> *"This is what the LORD says— your Redeemer, who formed you in the womb: I am the LORD, who has made all things, who alone stretched out the heavens, who spread out the earth by myself."*   —Isaiah 44:24

Do we really believe that God is our Creator? Every time we sin, we betray the fact that we wish it were not so. Sin is a denial of God as Creator. If we really felt, in our innermost being, that we owe all that we are, every second of the day, to our God, how could we even consider rebellion against the one who so mercifully grants to us breath and life? Sin is, truly, utter folly when we realize that God made us for His own purposes, and we are dependent upon Him every moment.

But, it is just that— sin— that tempts us to deny that God is our Creator, and for good reason! If we wish to live our own lives, utterly free from worrying about doing what is right in God's sight, free from caring about His will, His purposes in this world, then we must find some way of dismissing God's creative claims upon us! And this we do in many ways. We come up with scientific theories that remove God from the picture so that we don't have to deal with Him. We embrace philosophies that place man in the driver's seat and leave concepts of God to the weak or the cowardly. But most often, for the mass of humanity, we attempt to shove the thought out of our minds. We exclude God, and our responsibilities to Him, from our thinking, preferring to clutter our thoughts with this or that.

Why? What terrible secret, known to all, lies buried under our frantic denials? It is quite simple, and quite offensive. We are but creatures. God created us. He can do with us whatever He likes.

We have no say in the matter. Does not the potter have the right to do with the clay as he sees fit? And does not the just and righteous God have the perfect right to do with His creation as He sees fit? Certainly He does. But we hate this. We rebel against this. It strikes us to the heart, *but we know it is true.* We cannot escape our creatureliness. And to make matters worse, we know that we have rebelled against the very one who gives us the breath to breathe! We, as sinners, fear Him, and for good reason. We have treated Him with spite and hatred, and have slighted the honor of that majestic, awesome One to whom it is said in the highest court of heaven,

> *"You are worthy, our Lord and God, to receive glory and honor and power, for you created all things, and by your will they were created and have their being."* —Revelation 4:11

God created, and God owns, by right, all things. We are His. Often the Bible uses the terminology of kingship to express God's rule over men and the universe. He is the "King of glory" as the Psalmist declared:

> *Who is the King of glory? The LORD strong and mighty, The LORD mighty in battle.* —Psalm 24:8 [7]

The ancient king had almost unlimited power. The greater his realm, the greater his glory. Since God rules as King over all the world, and the heavens above, He is the most glorious King, the King of kings. As subjects, we owe to Him our complete loyalty and obedience. But kings do not simply sit upon their thrones. They rule. They act. God does as well. He is a *sovereign* ruler.

Knowledge Unlimited

> *See, the former things have taken place, and new things I declare; before they spring into being I announce them to you.* —Isaiah 42:9

The true God of the Bible has all knowledge. Indeed, when speaking of His understanding, the Psalmist said that it "has no limit" (Psalm 147:5). There is nothing that God does not know. Why? Quite simply, because there is nothing He didn't create! He made it, and sustains it, and therefore knows everything about it! In Isaiah 42:9 God claims that before things spring into being, He announces them to His people! This is not a God who is taken by surprises! God is not in heaven, anxiously waiting for things to happen on earth, so that He can react to those things. God does not react. One who reacts is one whose actions are being determined by outside circumstances. What happens in this world, as we shall see below, happens at the command of God. He is not the great *responder*, but the great *initiator*.

The complete knowledge of God extends to humanity as well:

> *For when I sit and when I rise; you perceive my thoughts*
> *from afar. You discern my going out and my lying down;*
> *you are familiar with all my ways. Before a word is on my*
> *tongue you know it completely, O LORD. You hem me in—*
> *behind and before; you have laid your hand upon me.*
> *Such knowledge is too wonderful for me, too lofty for*
> *me to attain.*   —Psalm 139:2-6

The Psalmist found the fact that God had absolute and complete knowledge of him, even to his most intimate thoughts, to be a great and wonderful thing, knowledge that was "too lofty for me to attain." He knew that God had hemmed him in behind and before. God guided his life by His hand. The Psalmist loved this. Do we? Only the heart that has been awakened by the Spirit of God could speak the words of the Psalmist. Do we desire to say them with full sincerity? If we are Christ's, we should.

If God has all knowledge, and is the Creator of all things, then the following fact becomes all too evident: there is no such thing as contingency in this universe. Nothing happens by chance. Why do we say this? If there was contingency, then God would not know the future. When a contingent action took place, which, before its taking place, was unsure, then God would gain new knowledge upon observing this action. He would change (denying immutability) and would grow in knowledge (denying omniscience). Furthermore, if contingency existed, then God would be left reacting to events rather than decreeing them. We have already seen that this is impossible. The God of the Bible has all knowledge, all power, all understanding.

Sovereign Ruler

"You are my witnesses," declares the LORD, "and my servant whom I have chosen, so that you may know and believe me and understand that I am he. Before me no god was formed, nor will there be one after me. I, even I, am the LORD, and apart from me there is no savior. I have revealed and saved and proclaimed— I, and not some foreign god among you. You are my witnesses," declares the LORD, "that I am God. Yes, and from ancient days I am he. No one can deliver out of my hand. When I act, who can reverse it?"   *—Isaiah 43:10-13*

The Scriptures are filled with testimonies to God's sovereign power. The question that ends Isaiah 43:13 is one that needs no answer. Every man should know, simply as part of reality itself, the answer to the question that is asked. When God acts, it is done. No power in heaven or in earth can stop Him from accomplishing His design. This is the testimony of the Scriptures from beginning to end. Read carefully, with great consideration, the following words:

Our God is in heaven; he does whatever pleases him.
                                        —Psalm 115:3

The LORD does whatever pleases him, in the heavens and on the earth, in the seas and all their depths. *—Psalm 135:6*

Do we really believe in such a God? Is God truly free to do whatever He desires? We know that what God desires is holy, just and right— He never acts contrary to His nature. But, do we really believe what the Bible teaches here? What one decides about the sovereign power and will of God now will determine the outcome of the rest of the discussion about the doctrines of grace. This is the watershed, the breaking point. If we assert God's absolute freedom and ability here, we will not be able to come back and limit Him when we become uncomfortable with His sovereign working in salvation!

> *For the LORD Almighty has purposed, and who can thwart him? His hand is stretched out, and who can turn it back?*
> —*Isaiah 14:27*

Note a vitally important truth that is proclaimed here in the 14th chapter of Isaiah. God has purposed something. When God purposes something, it is asked, "who can thwart him?" In typical Hebrew style, this thought is then repeated in the next line. God's purpose is paralleled with the stretching out of His hand. Why is this important? Because it tells us that when God desires to do something, when it is His purpose to do something, He will do it! Nothing can stop Him in accomplishing His purpose— and that includes, as we shall see, the will of man! If it were possible for God to purpose the salvation of a man, and be thwarted in that purpose, then this Scripture is shown to be false. Sadly, many of the gospel presentations in our world today make a mockery of this passage!

> *Remember the former things, those of long ago; I am God, and there is no other; I am God, and there is none like me. I make known the end from the beginning, from ancient times, what is still to come. I say: My purpose will stand, and I will do all that I please.*   —*Isaiah 46:9-10*

Here we see a number of the concepts we have been considering placed side-by-side. God is the unique Creator, the one who makes known the beginning from what is yet to come. He is the eternal God, who created time itself, and all those things which take place therein. Against the backdrop of such tremendous claims God asserts that His purpose will stand, and He will do all that He pleases. Nothing will stand in His way. All the attributes of God together form one perfect whole. While we may need to think for a while about God's uniqueness, and then turn our small minds to His eternity, and then to His creation, and then His sovereignty, this is only because we cannot even begin to comprehend the fullness of the revelation that God has given us. But the Word makes it clear in this and many other passages, that not one of God's attributes stands alone. His immutability is part of His eternity. His sovereignty is part of His being the Creator. Each attribute is but a certain facet of the beautiful, dazzling diamond that is the God of Israel. For the one who truly wishes to know God as He is, this is a wonderful truth. For those who wish to "edit" God, it is a terrible realization to discover that when one denies one aspect of God's being, the others fall right behind. God refuses to be molded to our image. We must accept Him as He is if we are ever to know ourselves as we truly are.

The Decrees of God

"Present your case," says the LORD. "Set forth your arguments," says Jacob's King. "Bring in your idols to tell us what is going to happen. Tell us what the former things were, so that we may consider them and know their final outcome.
Or declare to us the things to come, tell us what the future holds, so that we may know that you are gods. Do something, whether good or bad, so that we will be dismayed and filled with fear. —Isaiah 41:21-23

A number of the passages we have cited so far in our study of the nature of God have come from the book of Isaiah, particularly chapters 40 through 48. There is a good reason for this. It is in this wonderful section of Scripture that we encounter what has been called the "trial of the false gods." In it, Yahweh, the true God, challenges all other gods (which are, in reality, nothing but idols) to come with Him to the law-court. He calls

Israel as His witness (Isaiah 43:10), and subjects these "gods" to cross-examination.

In challenging the false gods to this contest of the law-court, many wonderful facts about the *true* God are brought to the fore. This is often the case. When two positions are brought into conflict, the result is often a clarification of the issues involved on both sides. When the true God challenges all pretenders to the name "God," we gain a unique insight into His nature. Truth is often seen best against the backdrop of error.

In Isaiah 41:21-23, Yahweh challenges the gods of the peoples to do two things. These two things are feats that only the true God can perform. The first is clear— they are to tell us the future. The second is not as easily noticed. They are challenged to tell us what the "former things" were, what their outcome was. That is, they are not simply to give a dry recital of past events, but they are challenged to reveal why things happened the way they did!

What does this tell us? Quite simply, it tells us that if the true God can tell us what has happened in the past, and why it happened, then it is obvious that nothing has ever happened that was without His purpose! Everything that takes place in this world does so for a purpose. And, since this is so (if it were not, how could God challenge others to do what He Himself cannot do?), then it follows that God Himself is the one who has decreed what will take place in the world, and in so doing, He is bringing about His purpose, His will.

All that happens in this world, even the small and seemingly insignificant things only happen at the decree of God. In eternity past God gave shape to creation by His decrees. What we see unfolding around us is simply the outworking of God's decrees, which is why the Apostle Paul describes God as the one "who works out everything in conformity with the purpose of his will" (Ephesians 1:11). As we will note in a later chapter, Paul in this passage speaks of the salvation of God's people. Here, in the very working out of the gospel plan itself, God is seen as the one who works out everything in conformity with His will. He has decreed the salvation of His people, He has decreed the weather for tomorrow afternoon. If we believe that God truly is in control of the weather, we must believe He has no less control over all else, including the actions, thoughts, and decisions of mankind!

Providence: Decrees in Action

Let all the earth fear the LORD; let all the peoples of the world revere him. For he spoke, and it came to be; he commanded, and it stood firm. The LORD foils the plans of the nations; he thwarts the purposes of the peoples. But the plans of the LORD stand firm forever. the purposes of his heart through all generations.   —*Psalm 33:8-11*

Providence is God's activity in the world. Yet, have we not said that God is not limited to time, that He is not experiencing a flow of events like we do? Yes, we have said that. Then what do we mean by God's activity in the world?

Of course, we are again using a human analogy to attempt to describe how it is that God is active in the world. Why do we do this? Because we are forced to by His revelation in the Scriptures. The Psalmist tells us that God "foils the plans of the nations" and "thwarts the purposes of the peoples." Of course, this is said simply in affirming that it is God's plans and purposes that stand firm, it is His will that will be accomplished.[8] So when God's purpose (a decree made in eternity *past*) comes to pass in time, we experience it as a function of our *present*. It looks to us, as time-bound creatures, like God is acting in time, acting in the same way we act,— in the past, present, and future modes of being.

God's providence is most certainly to be seen in the natural world, in weather, storm, fire or earthquake (Psalm 147:15-18). Even the ungodly man speaks of these things as "acts of God."

But the most striking examples of God's providential care for His creation can be seen in His working with men. For example, when Abimelech unwittingly took Sarah from Abraham in Genesis 20, he placed himself in grave jeopardy. Upon discovering Sarah's true identity, Abimelech became anxious and pleaded his innocence. God spoke to him in a dream, as we read:

> Then God said to him in the dream, "Yes, I know you did this with a clear conscience, and so I have kept you from sinning against me. That is why I did not let you touch her"
> —Genesis 20:6

Note what God says. "I have kept you from sinning against me." God actually intervened (from our perspective) and kept a man from sinning against Him.

Does the Bible really teach that God is so in control of the world that He is able to keep us from sinning against Him? Does the word really teach us that we, as creatures, are under the mighty hand of God? It most certainly does! Note these passages from the wisdom writer:

> In his heart a man plans his course, but the LORD determines his steps.   —Proverbs 16:9

> Many are the plans in a man's heart, but it is the LORD's purpose that prevails.   —Proverbs 19:21

> A man's steps are directed by the LORD. How then can anyone understand his own way?   —Proverbs 20:24

> The king's heart is in the hand of the LORD; he directs it like a watercourse wherever he pleases. —Proverbs 21:1

Another glowing example of God's providence in the affairs of men is to be found in His use of entire nations as instruments of chastisement and punishment upon Israel. Listen to what God says about the Assyrians who came down against Israel:

> Woe to the Assyrian, the rod of my anger, in whose hand is the club of my wrath! I send him against a godless nation, I dispatch him against a people who anger me, to seize and

*loot and snatch plunder, and to trample them down like
mud in the streets. But this is not what he intends, but this is
not what he has in mind; his purpose is to destroy, to put an
end to many nations.   —Isaiah 10:5-7*

The Assyrians were tremendously cruel people. They were
vicious in battle, and treated captive peoples with unparalleled
brutality. They cared nothing for the God of Israel. Yet, God
claims that He is the one sending the Assyrians against His
people. Not only this, but God tells us that this is not what the
Assyrian intends! The hordes of Assyrian soldiers were hardly
thinking about bringing righteous judgment down upon God's
people! It was the farthest thought from their mind! They just
enjoyed plundering, killing, and looting. Yet God was in control
of their activities. This mighty army was but a club in His hand,
and instrument of His wrath!

A great leader of the ancient world learned about God's sovereignty and providence first hand. Nebuchadnezzar, king of
Babylon, became prideful in heart, and God taught him a lesson. He took away his sanity for seven years. Daniel tells us:

*At the end of that time, I, Nebuchadnezzar, raised my eyes
toward heaven, and my sanity was restored. Then I
praised the Most High; I honored and glorified him who
lives forever. His dominion is an eternal dominion; his
kingdom endures from generation to generation. All the
peoples of the earth are regarded as nothing. He does as he
pleases with the powers of heaven and the peoples of the
earth. No man can hold back his hand or say to him:
"What have you done?"   —Daniel 4:34-35*

We do not read of Nebuchadnezzar pleading his "free will"
in the face of God, that is for certain! He acknowledged God for
who God was, and in so doing, saw himself in the proper perspective. He recognized his status as a creature, incapable of
disputing the decisions of the almighty God of creation! Would
that we all, without the necessity of the same extreme measures,
could see God as He is!

Theodicy: The Problem of Evil

In closing our brief examination of some of the important (and often forgotten) aspects of God's revelation concerning Himself, we must take the time to deal with the most obvious objection that is to be raised against what has come before. What of evil? If we say that God is all good, and that He hates sin and evil, and if we also say that nothing takes place outside of His sovereign decree, and that He has all power, why does evil exist? Does this not show that God is not completely sovereign, that He does not exercise complete control over all things?[9]

First, we gladly accept this question, for we feel that it is 1) forced upon us by the Bible's own teaching, and 2) we would much rather have to struggle with the existence of evil, trusting that God's purposes are just and holy in all things (even when we can't see all of His purposes ourselves) than to be left with the alternative. And what is the alternative? It is a God who is not in control, one who wishes that things could be different, but is powerless to bring this about. The heart is not drawn to worship a God who brought this world into existence but did not plan well enough to avoid the current situation. No, we will stay with the Scriptures and struggle with the existence of evil rather than accept such a deity as man would have us to worship.

> I am the LORD, and there is no other; apart from me there is no God. I form the light and create darkness, I bring prosperity and create disaster; I, the LORD, do all these things.   —Isaiah 45:5, 7

Here the Lord proclaims that He forms light and creates darkness. Light and darkness are opposites— complete opposition, total antithesis. So when He goes on to say, "I bring prosperity, and create disaster," these two terms are to be understood as antithetical as well. The Hebrew term "prosperity" is *shalom*. The other term used is *ra*, most often translated, as it is in the

King James Version, as "evil." However we translate the term, it is the complete opposite of peace, prosperity, well-being. It is to peace what darkness is to light. Upon saying this, Yahweh says, "I, the LORD, do all these things."

God has claimed responsibility. He is sovereign. Yet, He also says that He is holy and just. How can this be?

I believe that everything, ultimately, will result in the glory of God. The salvation of the elect, specifically, is said to result in the "praise of his glorious grace" (Ephesians 1:6). If the great act of salvation by God results in praise and worship, then it follows that all of creation itself— this entire drama unfolding around us— is meant to bring about the same end. God will be glorified in all things.

This means, of course, that evil itself will result in God's glory. How? We cannot always tell. We see such a small amount of the entire story. But should we not remember Joseph's words to his brothers in Genesis 50? After the death of Jacob, Joseph's brothers become fearful that he will now bring retribution upon them for having sold him into slavery years before. They come before Joseph and fall down in fear. But Joseph reassures them with these words:

> Don't be afraid. Am I in the place of God? You intended to harm me, but God intended it for good to accomplish what is now being done, the saving of many lives.
> —Genesis 50:19-20

The action of selling Joseph into slavery was, without question, an evil one. No one would argue this. Yet, Joseph says that God *intended* the action for good. God was working in the very same situation to bring about His intended purpose. The *motivation* of Joseph's brothers was evil; the *purpose* of God in the very same action was good and pure.

But there is one example that, I feel strongly, should be sufficient for those who love the Lord Jesus Christ. We find this example presented to us in the prayer of the Church in Acts:

> *Indeed Herod and Pontius Pilate met together with the*
> *Gentiles and the people of Israel in this city to conspire*
> *against your holy servant Jesus, whom you anointed. They*
> *did what your power and will had decided beforehand*
> *should happen...*   —Acts 4:27-28

The Church did not mis-speak this prayer. They acknowl-edged that what Herod and Pilate and the Jews had done to Jesus Christ in the crucifixion was exactly what God's power and will had decided beforehand should happen! But was not Pilate guilty in condemning Jesus? Of course! Was Herod free of con-demnation? No! Were the Jewish leaders acting with pure moti-vations, or were their hearts filled with hatred toward the Christ? The answer is obvious. Yet, in this obviously evil action of condemning, and murdering, the sinless, pure Lamb of God, we see God's hand! It did not take place merely with His per-mission, but at His bidding! The motivations of those involved were evil, of this there is no doubt. Yet, can we think of any greater example where God's motivations were any higher, any purer? Can we think of any single event that will bring about more good, and result in more glory to God, than the death of Christ as the perfect substitute for God's people? Surely not! So, if we can see that God could work in the death of Christ, and utilize evil men to bring about His purposes, why must we question that He is able to do so in the everyday circumstances of life? Surely, we may not see the obvious reasons behind God's actions as we see them at Calvary, but does this mean that we should question God's goodness or wisdom? Certainly not.

Conclusion

"The absolute, universal, and unlimited sovereignty of God
requires, that we should adore him with all possible humil-
ity and reverence. It is impossible that we should go to excess

in lowliness and reverence of that Being who may dispose of us to all eternity, as he pleases." [10]

I have taken a great deal of time and effort to attempt to begin the discussion in the only way that it can be— by pointing our eyes away from ourselves and toward the God who has revealed Himself in Jesus Christ. As we move into the discussion of the gospel, and as we examine the doctrines of grace, we will be forced again and again to remember what we have seen here. The gospel is the work of God. It will never contradict what we know to be true of God. It is consistent with Him and His nature. He is not one thing in His existence, and another in His works. This is, surely, the place where most of those who are going to get off of the train of our discussion will do so. The real difficult decisions will have to be made before turning to the next chapter. Is God sovereign or not? The Scriptures speak clearly and without question. Will we listen and obey?

> *"This is the stumbling-block on which thousands fall and perish; and if we go on contending with God about his sovereignty, it will be our eternal ruin. It is absolutely necessary that we should submit to God, as our absolute sovereign, and the sovereign over our souls; as one who may have mercy on whom he will have mercy, and harden whom he will." [11]*

3

Man in Sin:
A Hard Truth to Accept

I have often loved darkness, observed lying vanities,
forsaken thy given mercies, trampled underfoot thy beloved Son,
mocked thy providences, flattered thee with my lips,
broken thy covenant. It is of thy compassion that I am not
consumed. Lead me to repentance, and save me from despair;
Let me come to thee renouncing, condemning, loathing myself,
but hoping in the grace that flows even to the chief of sinners.
At the cross may I contemplate the evil of sin, and abhor it,
look on him whom I pierced, as one slain for me, and by me.
— The Valley of Vision

It is a necessity to now turn our attention from contemplating the tremendous God of creation to consider the plight and condition of man, the fallen creature. We know that man was created in the "image of God," and that in his original state man was good, just as God intended. But man did not remain in that state, and no one on earth today can be understood apart from the reality of the fall of man.

This chapter is not intended to be an exhaustive accounting of what the Bible teaches about man. Instead, we need to focus primarily on those topics that are relevant to the Reformed concept of *total depravity*. Let's start with a definition.

When we speak of total depravity, we are not in any way asserting that man is *as evil* as he could possibly be; or that your grandmother is actually an axe-murderer in disguise. In fact, no one has ever been as evil as they *could have been*, for God is actively restraining sin by reigning in the evil of man.

Total depravity speaks to the condition, and nature, of man. Basically, this doctrine teaches that *all aspects of mankind's character* has been touched by sin— no part of man's nature has escaped the pollution of sin. Man's mind, man's heart, his emotions, our will (Yes!, *our will*)— *every part* has been altered, changed, or damaged by sin. The effect of sin's curse is total.

Some Reformed writers like other names for this doctrine. One of the best alternatives (that even maintains the "TULIP" acrostic) is "total inability." This refers to the results of sin, especially in relationship to spiritual things. It speaks to the fact that the Bible teaches that man is incapable of doing what is right, pure, and good in God's eyes, since man is in sin. In fact, as we will see below, this extends even to the truth, taught by Jesus in John 6:44, that man is incapable of coming to Him unless God supernaturally intervenes in grace!

Talking about our sin is not a "comfortable" thing to do. It does not tend to make people feel good. You do not become tremendously popular by talking about man's *in*abilities, man's *in*capacities. We live in a humanistic age, where man's capacities and abilities are greatly touted from every corner, and, sadly, from many a pulpit as well. In that context it is obvious why the Reformed emphasis upon the sovereignty of God and the inability of man is not the message of the day. But we insist that this is what the Bible teaches. Let's turn to the Word of God, again with a commitment to reverence and obedience.

Sinful Man

The Scriptures are full of clear affirmations of the sinfulness of man. While we will see the clearest exposition of man's sin, and its effects, in Paul's writings, the testimony begins at the very beginning. Note the words of Moses:

"The LORD saw how great man's wickedness on the earth had become, and that every inclination of the thoughts of his heart was only evil all the time." —Genesis 6:5

Prior to the flood, mankind had reached great depths of sin and rebellion. The very thoughts of his heart, his innermost being, were continually evil. Some might think that this was a one-time affair— that after the flood, man somehow "improved." But this is not the case. Noah was just as effected by the fall as any other man, and evil continued to be the universal experience of man following the flood. Note the words of the Lord to Noah:

"Never again will I curse the ground because of man, even though every inclination of his heart is evil from child-hood." —Genesis 8:21

The prophet Jeremiah had a keen insight into the hearts of men. Listen carefully to some of his words:

"Can the Ethiopian change his skin or the leopard its spots? Neither can you do good who are accustomed to doing evil." —Jeremiah 13:23

The Ethiopian by nature has one kind of skin. He cannot by the exercise of his will, change the color of his skin. The leopard, in the same way, has spots that cannot be removed. So the sinner, who is accustomed to doing evil, cannot break the bondage of that evil by his own power. The result of man's enslavement to evil is his inability to do good. Yet, do we not fool ourselves into thinking that we are good? Yes, but this shows us the treachery of the sinful heart. As Jeremiah noted,—

"The heart is deceitful above all things and beyond cure. Who can understand it?" —Jeremiah 17:9

The wisdom writer, too, knew the true condition of man...

"The hearts of men, moreover, are full of evil and there is madness in their hearts while they live, and afterward they join the dead." —Ecclesiastes 9:3

...as did the Psalmist...

"Surely I was sinful at birth, sinful from the time my mother conceived me."—Psalm 51:5

Even from birth the wicked go astray; from the womb they are wayward and speak lies."—Psalm 58:3

Strong words indeed! The first inclination of our hearts in reading these words is to blunt their force or dismiss their meaning. We must realize that now we are talking about ourselves, and we are hardly objective when it comes to being convicted and convinced of our own evil! We have a vested interest in saying, "well, man isn't that bad." As long as this inclination is allowed to hold sway, we will never understand the necessity, nor the graciousness, of God's act of election. Indeed, I assert that 99% of the resistance that is presented by believers against the doctrine of predestination and election comes from one source: a grave misjudgment of the seriousness, and effect, of sin.[12]

Let us remember this important fact— *if* what the Bible says about man is true, then it follows that we are not in a position to make judgments about ourselves. That is, if our entire being, including our minds and even the intentions of our hearts, has been twisted and distorted by sin, then we are dependent upon an outside source of information— the Bible— for truth about our condition." I am not here addressing the truth that man from his creation, even before the fall, has been dependent upon God's revelation. We cannot trust our own judgment of what is "good" and "bad." We must have God's holy judgment. We may look upon someone and say, "my, what a good man," yet our judgment is not valid. Not only are we limited to what we can see (we cannot see the man's motives, his heart, his thoughts), but the standard of judgment that we use is based upon our own corrupted nature. We are evil ourselves, and that evil drags our standards down to the pit. We compare ourselves to ourselves, judging evil by evil, and the result in reality is little more than different levels of "bad," lesser or greater extents of evil. We must look to God to have the proper standard, for He alone is Holy. A wise man has said,—

> "Again, it is certain that man never achieves a clear knowledge of himself unless he has first looked upon God's face, and then descends from contemplating him to scrutinize himself....So it happens in estimating our spiritual goods. As long as we do not look beyond the earth, being quite content with our own righteousness, wisdom, and virtue, we flatter ourselves most sweetly, and fancy ourselves all but demigods. Suppose we but once begin to raise our thoughts to God, and to ponder his nature, and how completely perfect are his righteousness, wisdom, and power— the straightedge to which we must be shaped. Then, what masquerading earlier as righteousness was pleasing in us will soon grow filthy in its consummate wickedness. What wonderfully impressed us under the name of wisdom will stink in its very foolishness. What wore the face of power will prove itself the most miserable weakness. That is, what in us seems perfection itself corresponds ill to the purity of God.[14]

Every testimony to the sinfulness of man that we have seen so far has come from the Old Testament. Does the New Testament present the same truth? It most definitely does. The sinfulness of man, taught so clearly in the Old Testament, is assumed to be completely true by all the writers of the New. They not only accept this teaching, but expand upon it and discuss it in their own writings.

When one thinks of the book of Romans, such concepts as justification, faith, and adoption come to mind. This epistle of Paul gives to us a thought-out, structured argument of the gospel. Since this is so, we need to understand that Paul did not jump immediately into a discussion of such wonderful promises as our adoption as children of God, or the necessity of faith in Jesus Christ. He started out at a much more basic level. The first thing he talks about is sin, and the effect it has upon man. In fact, he spends the greater part of the first three chapters of the epistle on just this topic, and in so doing not only proves the universal sinfulness of man, but provides us with tremendous insights into— ourselves; tremendous, that is, if we are willing to really look at what he has to say.

"The wrath of God is being revealed from heaven against all the godlessness and wickedness of men who suppress the truth by their wickedness."   —Romans 1:18

Often we hear people say, "the God of the Old Testament was a God of wrath, but the God of the New Testament is a God of love." Such a statement shows an abysmal ignorance of both the Old and New Testaments. Here God's wrath is being revealed from heaven against the wickedness of men. What do these men do? They suppress the truth by their wickedness. One cannot suppress something that one does not have. Therefore, it is obvious that God has revealed Himself to man. This is exactly what Paul goes on to assert.

"Since what may be known about God is plain to them, because God has made it plain to them. For since the creation of the world God's invisible qualities— his eternal power and divine nature— have been clearly seen, being understood from what has been made, so that men are without excuse."   —Romans 1:19-20

God has revealed Himself through what He has created. Theologians call this "natural" or "general" revelation. We not only see irrefutable confirmation of God's existence in the beauty, order, and purpose of nature, but God has indelibly stamped the knowledge of His existence upon our souls. We know of God's "eternal power and divine nature" from what He has made. While sin may mask some of this knowledge, it does not destroy it. Paul asserts that the natural revelation of God is sufficient to hold men responsible for their actions, for their rebellion against God.

"For although they knew God, they neither glorified him as God nor gave thanks to him, but their thinking became futile and their foolish hearts were darkened. Although they claimed to be wise, they became fools and exchanged the glory of the immortal God for images made to look like mortal man and birds and animals and reptiles."
—Romans 1:21-23

Paul teaches that men knew God. What result should knowing God produce? We can answer that question by seeing what Paul accuses men of not doing. They do not glorify him as God, nor do they give thanks to Him. These two things men know to do from creation itself. Man knows in his heart that he should glorify God and give thanks to God. But it is just this truth that man suppresses. He does not give thanks, he does not give the glory due to his Creator. Instead, his very thinking becomes futile, empty, without reason. His foolish heart becomes darkened, without the light of truth. He claims wisdom, but in reality espouses the greatest foolishness. He exchanges the glory of God for idolatry, the worship of created things that he knows are not worthy of true worship. Any kind of activity that detracts from the glory of God is idolatry; any philosophy that does not have God at its center is idolatrous foolishness. While men may call such things "wise," they are in fact "foolish."

> *"Therefore God gave them over in the sinful desires of their hearts to sexual impurity for the degrading of their bodies with one another. They exchanged the truth of God for a lie, and worshiped and served created things rather than the Creator— who is forever praised. Amen."*
> —Romans 1:24-25

What does sin do to man? It *twists* him. Sinful man exchanges truth for a lie. He was made to worship and serve, but in his rebellion against God, he exchanges truth for a lie, and directs his natural urge to worship and serve *away* from God toward the creation itself. Rather than worshiping God, he worships what God has created.

This "exchange" of truth for a lie is vital to our understanding of man in sin. Sinful men hate the sovereignty of God. Why? Because they know that they are living a lie— a lie that is exposed when God's sovereignty is preached. Man has attempted to kick God off of His throne. In fact, in his impudent foolishness, man imagines himself sitting upon the throne! "It is my life, and I will do with it as I wish!" How many times have we heard this? Such ideas are a part of our sinful nature. We do not wish to serve the sovereign God, and the best way to avoid having to deal with Him is to imagine that He is subservient to us. We go so far as to think that God can be judged by our standards! We think we can bring God before our court and judge Him! Such foolishness comes from our sin. It comes from denying the Creator/creation distinction. We drag God down to our level so that we do not have to deal with Him. What does this have to do with the doctrines of grace? Quite simply, we must understand that our natural desire will not be to embrace the sovereignty of God and all that means. Not only will lost men hate what we have to say (since it exposes their creatureliness and therefore their rebellion against God, since they are, in fact, living as if they were not creatures!), but even the man who has been changed by the Spirit of God may struggle with the high claims of God found in Scripture. We must ask God to implant within our hearts by His Spirit a love for the truth, especially when that truth is so strongly opposed to the sin that we experience in our lives. We must ask God to help us to love Him as He is, not as we would like Him to be! How often do we do that?

Total Depravity Seen in Man's Inabilities

How radically depraved is man? How completely has sin changed him? Listen to the words of Paul:

> "As it is written: 'There is no one righteous, not even one;
> there is no one who understands, no one who seeks God.
> All have turned away, they have together become worthless;
> there is no one who does good, not even one.
> Their throats are open graves; their tongues practice deceit.
> The poison of vipers is on their lips.
> Their mouths are full of cursing and bitterness.
> Their feet are swift to shed blood; ruin and misery mark
> their ways, and the way of peace they do not know.
> There is no fear of God before their eyes.' " —Romans 3:10-18

The true extent of the effect of sin upon man can be seen in this chain of Old Testament passages. This section from Romans 3 provides the conclusion, the summing up, of Paul's entire discussion of the sinfulness of man. It is a machine-gun testimony, drawn from the Scriptures, to the wickedness of humanity. It is so overwhelming that many do not stop to ponder the statements themselves. Yet some very important truths are to be found by listening closely to what is said.

Paul begins by asserting that there is no righteous man, not even one. Sin is universal. Then he says that there is none who understands. Sin affects the understanding, the mind. As he said earlier, man's thoughts have become dark and futile.

Then we read a passage that seems to have fallen out of the vast majority of Bibles in our land today, so often is its teaching ignored: "there is...no one who seeks God." Literally, the original language has the phrase, "there is a God-seeker" preceded by the negative, "no." There is no God-seeker. There is no man seeking after God. Men do not seek after the true God of creation. We cannot think that all we have to do is tell folks the good news and they will just jump at the chance to follow God in obedience. We cannot spread the gospel with the idea that there are all sorts of folks out there who would really like to do God's will if they just knew how! No, lost man is doing everything in his power to stay away from the true God. Does this surprise you? Do you reply and say, "no, I know someone who is seeking God. They are really concerned about knowing the truth." May I suggest one of two possibilities? First, if they really are seeking God, then they are doing so because God has first moved in their life and has, in His grace, drawn them to Himself. Otherwise, I have to say that such a person may be seeking philosophical enlightenment, religiosity, the acclaim of men, or any number of other things that make them look like a God-seeker. But, unless God has moved in their lives, they are not seeking God.

Men have come up with all sorts of ways to avoid seeking

God. Humanism is a very good example. But the most prevalent throughout history has been, believe it or not, religion. Religion is a great way to avoid dealing with the true God. Create a system of beliefs that present to you a God of your own making, soothe your conscience by doing various "works" and undergoing certain "rituals," and all is well! That gnawing feeling that your "good works" mean nothing to the real and holy God will only bother you once in a while, and at that time you just go and get real religious for a while and the feeling will pass. The religions of men have one thing in common: idolatry. Religious worship of anything or anyone but the true God is idolatry. God has the right to define what is, and what is not, acceptable worship. Man, in his sin, does not want to give to God what is His due. So, he creates false systems of worship to hide him (so he thinks) from God. And did you note the final words of this passage from Romans? "There is no fear of God before their eyes." They have no awe, no sense of the glory of God. They have become hardened and senseless. Sinful men do not seek God. Paul goes on to say that they do no good, either. Here is another assertion that brings immediate response from men. "Do no good? That's ridiculous! All sorts of non-religious people do good!" Relatively speaking, that is true. But Paul is not speaking relatively. He is talking about what is good, and what is not, in the sight of God. God is not relative. He does not wink at sin. He sees our hearts, and knows our motivations. Nothing that man can do is ever pure and perfectly good as long as he remains in rebellion against his Creator. Man's inability to do good is seen in another passage from Paul:

> "As for you, you were dead in your transgressions and sins, in which you used to live when you followed the ways of this world and of the ruler of the kingdom of the air, the spirit who is now at work in those who are disobedient."
> —Ephesians 2:1-2

Dead in sin. Can dead men do good things? No, they cannot.

Dead men are dead.

I have often drawn from my own personal experience to illustrate the deadness of man in sin. My close friends wish I would come up with some other example than the one that follows, but I still think that it communicates the point with clarity. While in college I had a rather strange double-major. I majored in Bible, and I majored in Biology as well. In my junior year I was chosen as department fellow in Anatomy and Physiology. One of my duties in this position was to assist the head of the department in doing demonstrations for groups of high school students who would visit the campus. The demonstration we designed had two components. One involved using a "physiograph" and doing a demonstration of various physical responses to stimuli, etc. The professor, being smart, and outranking me, handled that part. The other component involved a demonstration of human anatomy using our two cadavers— yes, dead bodies. Strangely enough, we knew the actual first names of our cadavers— Willy and Clara. I recall spending seven hours on one Saturday alone demonstrating anatomy to high school students using ol' Willy and Clara.

I won't go into a whole lot of detail in recounting just how these demonstrations were run. I will say this, however. I could do anything I wanted to Willy and Clara. I could pull off the top of Clara's skull to demonstrate the brain. I could pull Willy's heart out to demonstrate the flow of blood in the arterial system. I could do absolutely anything to Willy and Clara. And you know what? They never once complained. They never once resisted me. Why? Well that is obvious, you say. They were dead. They had no ability to resist me. Exactly. That is the point.

The Bible says that we were dead in our trespasses and sins. DEAD! Not gravely ill, not tremendously weakened or impaired, but utterly dead. Finished. Stiffs. Spiritually speaking, we were Willys and Claras. God could have performed a demonstration of our spiritual anatomy and there would have been nothing we could do about it. Dead in sin.

This is why the lost man can do no "good" as Paul said earlier. While I hope that some students were helped in their understanding of anatomy by my demonstrations with the cadavers, Willy and Clara themselves were incapable of doing "good." They were dead. So were we, until God "made us alive in Christ." (Ephesians 2:4)

This is not the only place that Paul taught this. In Colossians 2:13 we also read of that time when we were dead in our sins. In both instances, Paul asserts this truth immediately prior to a discussion of God's action of salvation in Jesus Christ. Obviously, for him, sin must be understood to have a proper knowledge of the work of God in Christ Jesus.

Paul was not teaching something that was new or different. The Lord Jesus taught the same doctrine quite clearly in the synagogue at Capernaum in John Chapter 6. When the Jews grumbled at the tremendous claims He was making concerning Himself, Jesus said,—

> *"Stop grumbling among yourselves...No one can come to me unless the Father who sent me draws him, and I will raise him up at the last day."—John 6:43-44*

The Lord's words are plain and unmistakable. He directly asserts that no man is able to come to Him without the drawing of the Father. No man, in and of himself, has the ability to come to Christ. No man will voluntarily humble himself and submit himself to the Lordship of Jesus Christ outside of a work of supernatural grace in the heart. Jesus speaks of an incapacity on the part of man. The drawing of the Father is absolutely necessary. This was a hard saying for the people, for later in the same discourse, when Jesus again makes the same assertion (John 6:65), many of his disciples turn away from Him and stop following Him (John 6:66). Those who do not follow Christ, and who do not accept His words, are those that have not been drawn by the Father. Should someone assert that all men are drawn by the Father, it must be pointed out that the Lord Jesus did not believe that this was so. According to John 6:44, all who are drawn are also raised up by Christ at the last day ("the Father draws him...I will raise him up..."). Clearly, Jesus did not teach that all men would be saved, so it is impossible to understand John 6:44 in any way that would teach universalism. Quite clearly, the truth—

> *"The man without the Spirit does not accept the things that come from the Spirit of God, for they are foolishness to him, and he cannot understand them, because they are spiritually discerned."—1 Corinthians 2:14*

is to be found running throughout the Word of God.

The fact is— *man is completely dependent upon God.* He is utterly incapable of doing good, incapable of coming to Christ, incapable of accepting and understanding spiritual things, outside of the supernatural work of God by His Spirit.

Needy Men

When the Scriptures reveal to us what we should ask from God, we can learn from this what we lack or are missing. Surely, if we are to ask something from God, then it follows logically that we do not have that thing in and of ourselves. We must be dependent upon an outside source for certain things. A quick examination of some relevant passages shows how needy man is when it comes to spiritual things! Note the Apostle's prayer—

> *"I keep asking that the God of our Lord Jesus Christ, the glorious Father, may give you the Spirit of wisdom and revelation, so that you may know him better. I pray also that the eyes of your heart may be enlightened in order that you may know the hope to which he has called you, the riches of his glorious inheritance in the saints, and his incomparably great power for us who believe." —Ephesians 1:17-19*

Paul prays that Christians might receive the Spirit of wisdom and revelation, that is, the Holy Spirit of God. Why? The New International Version says "so that you may know him better." The literal rendering is "in a true knowledge of Him." To have true knowledge, real, full knowledge of God, we must have the Spirit. Paul further prays for all Christians that the "eyes" of our hearts might be enlightened. Our eyes are naturally dull and heavy, and we need the Spirit to open them and give us light. Paul desires that we might know the hope to which we have been called. In and of ourselves, we could not know this. Without God's help, we could not know the riches of His glorious inheritance in the saints, nor His incomparably great power for believers.

Is this the kind of prayer we hear often today? Do we sense our need so deeply that we pray for God to open our eyes so that we might have knowledge of Him and what He has done for us in the Gospel? Honestly— what do you hear more often: prayers for material blessing, or prayers that ask God to lift us up so that we might know Him? Do we not need to understand our poverty before we can have true riches— the riches that are ours in simply knowing God and understanding the grace that He has given us in Christ Jesus? When Paul wrote to the Colossians, he revealed the content of his prayers for them as well:

> *"For this reason, since the day we heard about you, we have not stopped praying for you and asking God to fill you with the knowledge of his will through all spiritual wisdom and understanding." —Colossians 1:9*

Paul knew what Christians really needed. They did not need money and houses and luxuries. They needed to know the will of God by having spiritual wisdom and understanding. Again, as we are asserting, this means that outside of God's giving it to us, we do not have spiritual wisdom nor understanding;—

> *"There is none who understands..." —Romans 3:11*

as Paul had emphasized to the Romans.

When we keep in mind the truth that if we are taught by Scripture to ask something of God, this then is something that we lack in ourselves, we find many more passages that will continually teach us the wisdom of humility. When we read Philippians 1:9, we will know that since Paul prayed that the Philippians' love would abound, that we, too, must seek for the ability to love as we ought, see 1 Timothy 1:14. Other passages will leap from the page and remind us, again and again, of our neediness.

Slaves to Evil

> To the Jews who had believed him, Jesus said, "If you hold to my teaching, you are really my disciples. Then you will know the truth, and the truth will set you free."
>   —John 8:31-32

Most Christians are familiar with this passage. Entire musicals have been based upon its words. Yet, do we really hear what the Lord says? When we proclaim the gospel to men, do we make it clear that they need to be set free? Or do we fear telling men that they are enslaved?

It is very instructive to notice what happened after the Lord spoke these words:

> "They answered him, 'We are Abraham's descendants and have never been slaves of anyone. How can you say that we shall be set free?' Jesus replied, 'I tell you the truth, everyone who sins is a slave to sin.' " —John 8:33-34

These Jews had simply "believed" in Jesus in a surface way. They did not have an abiding faith, the kind of faith that comes from God. They immediately rebelled when the truth of their own condition was revealed to them. They were so offended at being told that they were not free that they were willing to lie about their own condition. They were under the control of Rome at this time, yet they assert that they had never been slaves of anyone. Little has changed! If anyone dares to proclaim the truth that man is in slavery to evil, and that the concept of "free will" is a myth, they receive a very similar response from men! The Lord Jesus' response was clear and straightforward: anyone who sins is under slavery to sin. Only Jesus Christ can free a person from sin, so, outside of Him, there is no freedom at all.

A number of years after this encounter between the Lord Jesus and these would-be followers, Paul wrote to Timothy and spoke of the same kind of slavery. Speaking of the work of the minister in dealing with opposition he said—

> *"Those who oppose him he must gently instruct, in the hope that God will grant them repentance leading them to a knowledge of the truth, and that they will come to their senses and escape from the trap of the devil, who has taken them captive to do his will." —2 Timothy 2:25-26*

The minister is to gently instruct those who oppose the gospel, trusting that God will give repentance[14] and they will recognize their real condition. And what is that? They have been taken captive by the devil to do his will. This is the situation of all who oppose the gospel of Christ, even if that opposition is simply disbelief. John warned his beloved children—

> *"The whole world is under the control of the evil one."*
> *—1 John 5:19*

This is not the neurotic opinion of some persecuted religious minority. It is the sober, factual teaching of the Bible.

The Universality of Depravity

Finally, we must make a few short comments on the fact that sin, and its effect, is a universal condition of man. No one is outside of the charge of Scripture that all have sinned (Romans 3:23). Let's look at a few direct statements from God:

> *"When they sin against you— for there is no one who does not sin— and you become angry with them, and give them over to the enemy, who takes them captive to a land far away or near..." —2 Chronicles 6:36*

And this was said of God's people, not some pagan country with no knowledge of God!

If you, O LORD, kept a record of sins,
O Lord, who could stand?
But with you there is forgiveness;
therefore you are feared." —Psalm 130:3-4

"Do not bring your servant into judgment
for no one living is righteous before you." —Psalm 143:2

The Psalmist of Israel knew the sin of his heart. He knew that if God kept a record of sins, no one could possibly stand before Him. Every man will be found guilty, every man would have to hear the word of condemnation from God's lips. There is none living who is righteous before God— (that is, outside of God's mercy,— His forgiveness found only in Jesus Christ;)

"Who can say, 'I have kept my heart pure; I am clean and without sin?' " —Proverbs 20:9 *(see also Ecclesiastes 7:20)*

This is of course is another rhetorical question, one without an answer. Nobody can make such a claim truthfully, although to my amazement, many have made this very claim in my presence. If anyone does not know the evil of their own heart, it is without question that they have both—
1) shut out the truth of God and know nothing of His majesty,
2) do not know themselves at all.

No one is more blind than the one who does not even know his own sin. The great "Suffering Servant" passage confirms what we have seen above—

"We all, like sheep, have gone astray, each of us has turned to his own way; and the LORD has laid on him the iniquity of us all." —Isaiah 53:6

As we shall see later, the sacrificial work of Christ on the cross is a meaningless, empty thing if it is possible for anyone to stand before God spotless outside of the Lord Jesus.

"All of us have become like one who is unclean, and all our righteous acts are like filthy rags; we all shrivel up like a leaf, and like the wind our sins sweep us away." —Isaiah 64:6

When even our righteous deeds are filthy in God's sight, we know that we have nothing left to plead before God. We are completely dependent upon His mercy and grace.

Conclusion

"We have already made the charge that Jews and Gentiles alike are all under sin." —Romans 3:9

It certainly is not popular, or easy, to say what the Word says. But if we truly wish to proclaim the gospel of Christ, we must be clear from the start. We cannot compromise the truth about God without engaging in idolatry. And we cannot compromise the truth about the sinfulness, depravity, inabilities, and captivity of man without undercutting the entire work of Jesus Christ. The sovereignty of God and the sinfulness of man. If you have seen what the Bible teaches to this point, you will have tremendous difficulty disagreeing with what comes after this. From this point on, each and every point of the doctrines of grace will flow necessarily, logically, Biblically, from what came before. I assert that if a person truly and fully accepts the absolute sovereignty and providence of God, and the sinfulness and depravity of man in sin, the other doctrines of unconditional election, specific redemption, irresistible grace, and the final perseverance of the saints will follow naturally.

We now turn to God's means of bringing sinful, dead men unto Himself. We move back into eternity, to the very counsel of the Trinity, and the decree of election.

4

The Grace of God in Salvation

"Therefore we must guard against depriving believers of anything disclosed about predestination in Scripture, lest we seem either wickedly to defraud them of the blessing of their God or to accuse and scoff at the Holy Spirit for having published what it is in any way profitable to suppress." — *John Calvin*

In 1689, a group of Baptists gathered in London, and presented to the world a statement of their faith in response to those who were accusing them of heresy and unorthodoxy. Here is some of what they had to say in the third chapter of their confession of faith:

"Although God knoweth whatsoever may or can come to pass upon all supposed conditions, yet hath he not decreed anything because he foresaw it as future, or as that which would come to pass upon such conditions.

Those of mankind that are predestined to life, God, before the foundation of the world was laid, according to his eternal and immutable purpose, and the secret counsel and good pleasure of his will, hath chosen in Christ unto everlasting glory, out of his mere free grace and love, without any other thing in the creature as a condition or cause moving them thereunto.

As God hath appointed the elect unto glory, so he hath, by the eternal and most free purpose of his will, foreordained all the means thereunto; wherefore they who are elected, being fallen in Adam, are redeemed by Christ, are effectually called unto faith in

Christ, by his Spirit working in due season, are justified, adopted, sanctified, and kept by his power through faith unto salvation; neither are any other redeemed by Christ, or effectually called, justified, adopted, sanctified, and saved, but the elect only.

The doctrine of this high mystery of predestination is to be handled with special prudence and care, that men attending the will of God revealed in his Word, and yielding obedience thereunto, may, from the certainty of their effectual vocation, be assured of their eternal election; so shall this doctrine afford matter of praise, reverence, and admiration of God, and of humility, diligence, and abundant consolation to all that sincerely obey the gospel.

Some Baptists who read this might be more than just a little surprised to know that this is part of their heritage. Yet, not so long ago, the vast majority of Protestant denominations were willing to confess the truth that God has elected some to salvation, and others He has not. Surely, today, it is quite unpopular to confess this truth, but the Word of God, the Bible, is filled with this teaching. God's freedom of choice, as the Creator of all things, is everywhere in Holy Scripture.

> To the LORD your God belong the heavens, even the highest heavens, the earth and everything in it. Yet the LORD set his affection on your forefathers and loved them, and he chose you, their descendants, above all the nations, as it is today ."
>
> —Deuteronomy 10:14-15

The people of Israel knew that they were "chosen" by God. They were the objects of God's love, God's mercy. He did not choose them because they were "better" than anyone else; they did not draw God's favor by being a mighty nation, or an especially righteous nation. No indeed. As the Bible records,—

> "The LORD did not set his affection on you and choose you because you were more numerous than other peoples, for you were the fewest of all peoples. But it was because the LORD loved you and kept the oath he swore to your forefathers that he brought you out with a mighty hand and redeemed you

from the land of slavery, from the power of Pharaoh king of Egypt. Know therefore that the LORD your God is God; he is the faithful God, keeping his covenant of love to a thousand generations of those who love him and keep his commandments." —Deuteronomy 7:7-9

The basis of God's choice of Israel was simply His love. It was His decision, His will. This leaves no room whatsoever for boasting on the part of Israel. Yes, Israel became complacent and did indeed boast. But they had no reason to do so. Some did not listen closely to what the Psalmist said:

*"Blessed are those you choose and
bring near to live in your courts!
We are filled with the good things of your house,
of your holy temple." —Psalm 65:4*

Despite man's ability to twist the gracious choice of God into a basis for boasting, the fact remains that God is free, as the sovereign of the universe, to choose who He will, and who He will not, draw unto Himself. This truth is seen in His dealings with Israel.

Unconditional Election

God's election of men unto salvation is unconditional. What does this mean? Why is it important? We are now in a position to understand this vital truth of God's Word, for we have examined the twin pillars of God's absolute sovereignty and man's complete inability. God's choice must not be conditioned upon the actions of men for two obvious reasons: first, this would make God the responder rather than the sovereign initiator; secondly, man is dead in sin, and therefore is incapable of "doing" anything that would provide a foundation for God's action in the first place.

The most common "explanation" of God's election[16] is:

Since God— 1) knows the future; and 2) "sees" who will believe in Him, He then 3) elects that individual to salvation based on that knowledge.[17] By this argument, the concept "free will" is (seemingly) affirmed, and the sovereignty of God is no longer contemplated to limit the freedom of man. But does such an "explanation" have merit?

It does not in the least! Firstly, it assumes a number of things that we have already seen are false. It assumes that man can, as an exercise of his own free choice, "choose" God. Secondly, it does not properly comprehend *why* God has knowledge of the future. God's knowledge of the future is related to His role as Creator— He knows the future because He ordained the future! The course of the future is certain because God created it. Therefore God's election of an individual cannot possibly be based upon the previous action of the creature, which God merely takes note of by peering down the corridors of time, for this would result in God being subject to the whim of His creation. Lastly, the whole concept is entirely backwards from what Scripture clearly teaches— that God's sovereign choice in election *is* why we "make our choice" for God. Our faith, our belief, as we shall see, is the effect of God's election (the cause), and *not* the other way around.

The Lord Jesus on Election

When the doctrine of election is discussed, most people think immediately of the discussions provided by the Apostle Paul in such great passages as Romans 8-9 and Ephesians 1. But before Paul wrote of God's electing grace, the Lord Jesus taught the same doctrine, and that with just as much clarity.

> *"All that the Father gives me shall come to me, and whoever comes to me I will never drive away." —John 6:37*

In His great discourse in the synagogue at Capernaum, the Lord Jesus asserted that *all* that the Father gives to Him will come to Him. He did not say that most of them would come to Him, nor that the Father would do his best to make sure that a majority of them would come to Christ, but that *all* that the Father gives to Him will, without fail or exception, come to Him.

How can we understand these words, other than to simply

and humbly accept the truth of God's electing grace? The Father chose whom He would, and would not, give to the Son. Those who are given to the Son will come to the Son, and believe in Him, and the Son will never, ever drive them away. Those that are *not* given to the Son by the Father will *not* come to the Son (John 6:44).* In either case, man is not the deciding factor, God is. Yes, man believes on Christ and looks on Him (John 6:40), but this is preceded by the clear statement that the decision of God determines who will look, who will believe. God is always in charge, God is always sovereign. We cannot say that we chose God; we must always affirm that any faith we have in God is the result of His mercy and grace. As Christ said to the disciples, "You did not choose me, but I chose you and appointed you to go and bear fruit" (John 15:16). We love Him because He first loved us.

> "All things have been committed to me by my Father. No one knows the Son except the Father, and no one knows the Father except the Son and those to whom the Son chooses to reveal him ." —Matthew 11:27

Who knows God the Father? Of course, the Father is known perfectly and completely by the Son. Can just anyone have knowledge of the Father? No, to know the Father one must go through the Son. The Son is the one who reveals the Father, explains Him, makes Him known (John 1:18). So the Son must will to reveal the Father before the Father can be known. Will all know the Father? No, many will perish in disbelief. Did the Son will to reveal the Father to those who so perish, but failed in His task of revelation? Surely not. The Son reveals the Father to those who are His own, to those who have been given to Him by the Father, just as Jesus said in prayer to the Father,—

---

*Also read *Drawn By The Father* by James White for a complete study of this passage. See the additional suggested reading section at the back of this book to obtain your copy.

"I have revealed you to those whom you gave me out of the world. They were yours; you gave them to me and they have obeyed your word." —John 17:6

The Lord Jesus believed and lived all the teachings of the Old Testament, all the truths of God that are revealed therein. He believed in the sovereign God of Isaiah 43:13 and Isaiah 45:7. He did not in the least bit change or alter the faith that was revealed through the prophets of old. God is sovereign in all things, and in salvation as well.

Appointed to Eternal Life

The missionary experience of the Church reveals God's sovereign electing grace as well. When Paul and Barnabas preached the gospel at Pisidian Antioch, the Jews opposed their message, and spoke abusively about them. In response, they boldly asserted that they were now turning to the Gentiles, for the gospel message is for all men, Jew and Gentile alike. What was the result of their announcement?

"When the Gentiles heard this,
they were glad and honored the word of the Lord;
and all who were appointed for eternal life believed."
—Acts 13:48

Who believed the gospel message? Was it simply anyone and everyone who decided to believe it? No, for the Gentiles "were glad" at the message they heard. Do unregenerate, spiritually dead people rejoice at the sound of the gospel? They also honored the word of the Lord. Do those who are enemies of God[18] honor His word? Certainly not! So who believed? "All who were appointed for eternal life believed"; but who appoints to eternal life? Do men appoint themselves? Of course not, that's an impossibility. God appointed them to eternal life, and they believed as a result of God's election. When Paul wrote to the church at Thessalonica, he mentioned one of the reasons of his thankfulness before God:

"But we ought always to thank God for you, brothers loved by the Lord, because from the beginning God chose you to be saved through the sanctifying work of the Spirit and through belief in the truth. He called you to this through our gospel, that you might share in the glory of our Lord Jesus Christ."
—*2 Thessalonians 2:13-14*

The Thessalonian believers were "loved by the Lord." In what way? They were the objects of God's special grace. Paul believed that "from the beginning" God had chosen them. Chosen them for what? To be saved. How? Through the sanctifying work of the Spirit and through belief in the truth. God chose them, and that at the beginning. This was not a choice that came about "down the road," so to speak. God also chose the means by which they were to be saved. They were to be sanctified by His Spirit, and they were to believe in the truth. Sanctification and belief, then, are the means God has chosen, and therefore the fact that we are sanctified and that we believe is the result of God's choice, God's election. Those who assert that we choose to believe, and then God, foreseeing this human action, elects us, have it completely backwards. God chooses, we, in response, believe. We are called unto the Father through the gospel of Jesus Christ, not through any action— or decision— of our own. We do believe, we do trust, we do follow— but all as a response to His gracious choice. As Paul had said in his earlier letter to the Thessalonians:

"For God did not appoint us to suffer wrath but to receive salvation through our Lord Jesus Christ." —*1 Thess. 5:9*

Peter, too, in his exhortation of believers, made mention of the same truths. In his first epistle we read—

"Peter, an apostle of Jesus Christ, to God's elect, strangers in the world, scattered throughout Pontus, Galatia, Cappadocia, Asia and Bithynia, who have been chosen according to the foreknowledge of God the Father, through the sanctifying work of the Spirit, for obedience to Jesus Christ and sprinkling by his blood." —*1 Peter 1:1-2*

The Bible often uses the simple term "elect" or "called" as a proper name of the people of God, so basic is this truth in Scripture. Peter writes to God's "elect," and describes them as those "who have been chosen according to the foreknowledge of God the Father." Immediately someone will wish to stop the conversation and point out that "foreknowledge" is simply God's knowledge of future events, and this clearly shows, then, that God's choice is based upon future events. But this surely is not so. Foreknowledge, especially as it is used here and by Paul in Romans 8:29, does not mean a bare knowledge of future events. Instead, a study of the word[19] reveals that it refers to a decision on God's part to enter into close, personal relationship with someone. God's "knowing" of us is a personal thing— Scripture reveals that persons, not events, are foreknown. It is this decision on God's part that is at the foundation of the decree of election. We shall see more of this truth when we examine the first chapter of the book of Ephesians.

Paul: A Recipient of the Grace of God

Quite possibly the book 2 Timothy was the last work, or most certainly one of the last, written by the Apostle Paul. After many years of ministry, struggling against opposition both within and without the Church, the aging missionary to the Gentiles writes with deep emotion and tenderness to the young pastor in Ephesus. Right at the beginning of this letter of encouragement, Paul speaks to Timothy's heart, and in so doing, shows to us how central God's electing grace is to the Christian life:

> "So do not be ashamed to testify about our Lord, or ashamed of me his prisoner. But join with me in suffering for the gospel, by the power of God, who has saved us and called us to a holy life— not because of anything we have done but because of his own purpose and grace. This grace was given to us in Christ Jesus before the beginning of time, but it has now been revealed through the appearing of our Savior, Christ Jesus, who has destroyed death and has brought life and immortality to light through the gospel.

*And of this gospel I was appointed a herald and an apostle
and a teacher. That is why I am suffering as I am. Yet I am
not ashamed, because I know whom I have believed, and
am convinced that he is able to guard what I have entrusted
to him for that day."*

—2 Timothy 1:8-12

In encouraging Timothy, Paul speaks of the God who saved
us, and who called us to a holy life. Why did God do this? Certainly not for anything we did! Instead, the basis of God's saving work is "his own purpose and grace." No election based
upon our actions to be found here! Paul speaks of God's grace,
which was given to us in Christ Jesus before the very beginning
of time itself! Before creation, God set His love and mercy upon
us in Christ Jesus. Before we had done anything— before creation even came into existence— God chose us, and granted to
us grace in His Son Jesus Christ. And we must not miss the importance of what Paul says in verse 11, for having just presented
the sovereign grace of God in eternity past, he says, "And of *this
gospel* I was appointed a herald...." The truth of God's grace *is*
the gospel, the gospel for which Paul was willing to suffer! This
is not some side-issue that can be dismissed as a "non-essential"! It involves the very definition of the gospel message itself.

The two greatest, most elaborate discussions of the doctrine
of election are to be found in Paul's epistles to the Ephesians and
the Romans. We begin with the letter to the Ephesians. Here, in
the first chapter, Paul breaks into a great anthem of praise and
worship, and the substance of this section revolves around God's
great grace in bringing men unto salvation. Read these words
carefully, and consider well their meaning in light of what has
come before:

*"Praise be to the God and Father of our Lord Jesus Christ,
who has blessed us in the heavenly realms with every
spiritual blessing in Christ. For he chose us in him before
the creation of the world to be holy and blameless in his
sight. In love he predestined us to be adopted as his sons*

through Jesus Christ, in accordance with his pleasure and
will— to the praise of his glorious grace, which he has freely
given us in the One he loves. In him we have redemption
through his blood, the forgiveness of sins, in accordance
with the riches of God's grace that he lavished on us with
all wisdom and understanding. And he made known to
us the mystery of his will according to his good pleasure,
which he purposed in Christ, to be put into effect when the
times will have reached their fulfillment— to bring all
things in heaven and on earth together under one head,
even Christ. In him we were also chosen, having been
predestined according to the plan of him who works out
everything in conformity with the purpose of his will."
                                            —Ephesians 1:3-11

There is so much in this passage, and we are so dizzied by
the heights to which we are taken, the glorious mysteries that
are presented before our wondering eyes, that I have often found
it necessary to ask a series of questions in an attempt to clarify
the important issues that might otherwise be missed.

We start out with praise to God for what He has done. What
did He do? He blessed us with every spiritual blessing in Christ
Jesus. Everything in this passage will be "in Christ," "in him," "in
the One he loves." Christ is central in all of salvation. Next, we
are told that God chose. Whom did He choose? He chose us. We
are the objects of His election, His choice. How were we chosen?
In Christ. When were we chosen? Before creation. Was there a
purpose to our being chosen? Yes, that we might be holy and
blameless in the sight of God. What else did God do? He predestined. How did He predestine? In love. Who or what did He
predestine? Us. Did God predestine a plan or a people? A people.
And what is the purpose of His predestination? That we be
adopted as his sons. How can we be adopted as His sons? Only
through Jesus Christ. This is in accordance with what? God's
pleasure and will. Since it is in accordance with God's will (God's
will, not man's will), what is the result? It is to the praise of his
glorious grace. How have we received this grace? Did we earn it,

or force God to give it to us by our works, or by our "choosing" Him? No, God freely gave this grace to us in the One he loves, in Jesus Christ.

So far we have seen that God is the one doing everything in this passage. God chooses, God adopts, God gives grace. It is God who is praised, God's grace that is glorified. But there is more. We are told that we have redemption. How? In Christ. How are we redeemed? Through his blood. What does redemption mean? The forgiveness of sins. How can this be? It is in accordance with the riches of God's grace. What has God done in grace? He has lavished it upon us with all wisdom and understanding. What else has God done? He made known to us the mystery of his will according to his good pleasure. And what does this involve? The bringing together of all things in heaven and on earth in Christ. And how do we fit into His will? We were also chosen in him. How? We were predestined according to the plan of God. How does Paul describe God in this passage? As the one who works out everything in conformity with the purpose of his will.

This tremendous passage reveals eternity past and eternity future. It spans the entirety of creation, and speaks of God's purpose in creating all that is. It would be enough just to get a glimpse of the Eternal One's purposes, but to find ourselves in the middle of God's plan, and to be the recipients of God's grace, is almost beyond words! Do we dare dismiss the words of Scripture when they call us to think so far beyond ourselves? Surely we must show reverence and awe in approaching a passage such as this, and our hearts should be filled with thankfulness at having the tremendous opportunity to know such things, but since the Spirit of God has deemed it proper to reveal these wonders, can we possibly ignore them because they are so challenging? We cannot!

Paul informs us that we were chosen in Christ Jesus before, literally, "the foundation of the world." Every man who truly and sincerely names the name of Christ does so because, in eternity past— before the earth existed or the sun rose for the first time— God chose him, elected him in grace. This is why God is praised for salvation, for He, and He alone, is the one responsible for salvation! There is no room for boasting, for the redeemed man is the object of God's grace, and that for no merit of his own. God receives all honor, glory, and praise, for He alone is Savior.

God has a purpose in bringing each one of the elect to salvation. First, He chose us so that we would be "holy and blameless in His sight." Obviously then, the means by which God accomplishes this (the substitutionary atonement of Christ which takes away our sins), was part of God's plan from the very beginning. Second, it was God's desire that the entire action of creation, and specifically the salvation of God's people, would result in the "praise of His glorious grace." God's glory is seen, and magnified, by His role as Savior. And third, Paul will remind the Ephesians that God had a plan for their lives as well:

> "For we are God's workmanship, created in Christ Jesus
> to do good works, which God prepared in advance for us
> to do."   —Ephesians 2:10

God created His people. He formed and fashioned them in Christ Jesus, and He purposed that they would be a people "zealous for good works" (Titus 2:14). He "prepared in advance" these good works, and they are part of His divine will and plan. God's glory is further seen in the fact that He is changing self-centered, sinful creatures into people who do good works— not, of course, to gain salvation, but because they know their Savior and their total dependence upon Him.

It would seem that the Bible could not be any plainer than this. Ephesians 1:11, for example, is so clear, so understandable, that to miss its teaching would seem inexcusable. We were chosen in Christ, predestined in accordance with the will of the Almighty, the one who is working out *everything* in accordance with the purpose of His will. This is fully consistent with what the Bible teaches about God's nature, as we have seen. It is absolutely demanded by what the Bible teaches about fallen man, for how else could we possibly be saved? If God had simply created a "plan," and then left it up to us, who would have been saved? Quite simply, no one at all! Rather, the Bible is clear and unmistakable in its teaching. But, we will not linger here in Ephesians 1, for there is yet more testimony to be heard.

The Golden Chain of Redemption

"And we know that in all things God works for the good of those who love him, who have been called according to his purpose. For those God foreknew he also predestined to be conformed to the likeness of his Son, that he might be the firstborn among many brothers. And those he predestined, he also called; those he called, he also justified; those he justified, he also glorified."   —Romans 8:28-30

Most Christians are more than familiar with Romans 8:28. When tragedy strikes, when death visits a family, this passage is often on the lips of those who seek to console and comfort, and well it should be. Yet, we must remember that the God who is here described is the God who "works for the good of those who love him" in all things. This is the God of Isaiah, the God of sovereignty. If God is not in charge of all things, and if His will is often thwarted by the actions of men, this passage has little meaning, and less ability to comfort.

That Paul understood this is seen in what he goes on to say in verses 29 and 30. He lays out a series of actions, all done by God, that, while certainly not exhaustively describing the actions of God in salvation, give us a clear framework upon which to work in thinking about the gospel. Writers have often referred to this as the "golden chain of redemption." Here are the elements of the chain—

Foreknowledge > Predestination > Calling > Justification > Glorification

The process starts with God's gracious choice to enter into relationship with us— this is His foreknowledge. This results in His predestination of those who are foreknown. They are predestined to salvation, or, as Paul mentions here, adoption into the family of God, resulting in conformity to the image of Christ. Some have attempted to say that all that is predestined is the plan whereby we are conformed to the image of Christ; that is, all that God has predestined is that everyone who believes in Christ will be conformed to His image. But the passage does not say this at all. Those who are foreknown are a people, not a plan. Plans are not conformed to the image of Christ. And Paul told the Ephesians that it was people who were called and predestined, not plans (Ephesians 1:11).

Those who are predestined are also called, and justified, and glorified. Now we might well ask a very important question here: how is this passage understood by those who reject the Reformed view of salvation? Can anyone consistently interpret this passage without coming to recognize God's sovereign grace?

One group is able to do so— universalists. Those who believe that everyone will be saved can consistently interpret this passage. They would say that all were foreknown, all were predestined, all were called, all were justified, and, in the end, all will be glorified. But, of course, universalism is directly contradictory to many other statements in Scripture, so we need not pause long on their position.

What of the Arminian, the standard evangelical of today? Examining most modern preaching by the standard of this passage is quite educational. Most would say that only some are foreknown, because God foresees their faith. They would say that only some are predestined, again because of God's being limited in His election by the actions of men in believing in Him. This clearly reduces the term "predestined" to something that is nearly meaningless. Be that as it may, most would argue that all are called, but only some are justified, and that only because they believe by an act of their own "free will." So, obviously, since only some are justified, then only some are glorified as well.

Only the Reformed position can provide a consistent interpretation of the passage that does no harm to the text, but flows naturally from the words of Scripture. Only the Reformed view can allow each of these actions to be wholly of God, completely the result of His will.

The Potter's Rights

The ninth chapter of the book of Romans contains some of the strongest language in all of Scripture. I have actually had people get up and walk out of Bible study classes when I simply read this passage (let alone when I discussed what it teaches). Scholars in modern times have done everything in their power to blunt the force of this chapter. Most of the time it is asserted that Paul is speaking only of nations, not of people. But an honest examination of the passage does not allow any deflection of the strong statements, the clear doctrine.

> *"Not only that, but Rebekah's children had one and the same father, our father Isaac. Yet, before the twins were born or had done anything good or bad—* **in order that God's purpose in election might stand:** *not by works but by him who calls— she was told, "The older will serve the younger." Just as it is written: "Jacob I loved, but Esau I hated."*   —Romans 9:10-13 (emphasis added).

Paul begins with an example from the Old Testament. He illustrates the basic fact that God's purpose in election *must* be accomplished, and *will* be accomplished. He points out that before the twins Jacob and Esau had done anything— *good or bad,* God had revealed what His purpose was going to be— that *Esau would serve Jacob* (rather than the other way around which was the established rule). God's election is not, Paul says, based upon works, but upon the will of the one who calls, that is, God.[20] It was God's will to accomplish His purpose through Jacob, not Esau, and nothing could change that.

Immediately we are repelled by this act of sovereignty, and say, "But that isn't fair to Esau! God isn't being just." In fact, we should note all through Romans 9 the objections that are raised, and answered, by Paul, and ask ourselves this question: whose side are we on? If we are raising the same objections to Scriptural truth that are presented here, what does this tell us? The vast majority of those who reject God's predestination and election, and man's dependence upon sovereign grace, use the exact same objections to those doctrines that are raised here! The first objection is raised and answered by Paul:

> "What then shall we say? Is God unjust? Not at all! For he says to Moses, 'I will have mercy on whom I have mercy, and I will have compassion on whom I have compassion.' "
> —Romans 9:14-15

How does Paul answer the objection? He reminds his readers of the fact that God is not bound to have mercy and compassion on anyone. God's mercy and compassion is reserved for those upon whom He wishes to bestow it. God's grace cannot be demanded by anyone. This is one of the most common misunderstandings of men, whether Christian or not. God does not have to save anyone. He does not have to be merciful. We are sinners. We are condemned. God could, if He willed, leave us in our sin, and simply execute justice upon us. We must never forget this. If God saves one man— just one— this is mercy and grace that is undeserved. Grace, if it is to be grace at all, must come from the free decision of God to bestow it upon an unworthy object— sinful men. If God has to be gracious, then we are no longer talking about grace. We cannot say, "it is not fair for God to be gracious to one and not another," because grace is not a part of "fair." What is fair would be justice, and in the case of sinners, that would be nothing but punishment.

It is somewhat like a governor who pardons one of the hundred men on death row. The governor has the power to make the pardon. The governor is under no obligation to pardon anyone, as everyone on death row has justly been condemned and deserves the punishment they are receiving. But if the governor pardoned one man, would we have any right to complain and say that he was being "unfair" by not pardoning all the condemned criminals? Of course not. In the same way, we are simply thinking muddled thoughts when we accuse God of being "unfair" when He exercises His free grace in calling some undeserving, condemned rebels unto Himself, and leaving others to their just punishment. Paul goes on:

> "It does not, therefore, depend on man's desire or effort, but on God's mercy. For the Scripture says to Pharaoh: "I raised you up for this very purpose, that I might display my power in you and that my name might be proclaimed in all the earth." Therefore God has mercy on whom he wants to have mercy, and he hardens whom he wants to harden."
> —Romans 9:16-18

It is obvious that Paul is here talking about individuals and not nations. What does "man's desire or effort" have to do with nations? God's mercy, not man's desire (will) or effort, is the final authority. All the striving of man (if men would even strive for acceptance in God's sight, which is most certainly not true) means nothing in the sight of God. Without God's mercy, there is no hope.

As an illustration of this, Paul reminds his readers of Pharaoh. God told Pharaoh in Exodus 9:16 that He had raised him up for a purpose. And what was that purpose? God desired to display His power so that His name would be proclaimed in all the earth. Therefore, Paul asserts, God will have mercy on whom He desires to have mercy, and He will harden whom He desires to harden.

We stop right here and say, "wait a minute— I simply will not accept such a concept. My God is fair, and this God of whom you speak is most definitely not." But let's think closely about our feelings. First, we look at Pharaoh and say, "Poor fellow. God really mistreated him." But such is hardly the case. We feel like siding with Pharaoh because we share something in common with him— we are sinners, just as he. We do our best to dismiss the fact that sinners have no claim on God's mercy. We forget that if God allows a sinner to exist for one instant after each and every act of sin, He is being gracious and merciful to them. And, on an even more basic level, we hate the fact that God can do with us as He pleases, sinner or not. We are creatures— *His* creatures, and He can dispose of us as He pleases. If He wants Pharaoh to perform a certain function in bringing about a display of God's power, we have absolutely, positively no grounds upon which to complain. God is God, and we are not.

Finally, the real question that must be asked of those who claim to be Christians is this: do we really feel that a display of God's power, and the proclamation of His name— in short, the glory of God— is more, or less important than a single individual human being? How important is the glory of God to us? If we are honest, we have to admit that God's glory is not the highest priority on our list. It should be. We must pray that God would make us like Christ in always seeking His glory. But when we look at this passage, and combine all the sinful attitudes that we have— our downplaying of our own sin, our dislike of the sovereignty of God, our woeful lack of love for the glory of God— we understand where our objections are coming from, and why they are, in fact, nothing but sinful attitudes. Paul knew this, for he raises the very same objection—

> "One of you will say to me: 'Then why does God still blame us? For who resists his will?' But who are you, O man, to talk back to God? 'Shall what is formed say to him who formed it, "Why did you make me like this?"' 'Does not the potter have the right to make out of the same lump of clay some pottery for noble purposes and some for common use?'"
>
> —Romans 9:19-21

Paul had obviously spoken of God's sovereign election before, and had heard all the standard objections, too. If God raises men up for particular purposes, and disposes of them as He wishes, how then can anyone be judged? How can God hold us responsible? We obviously cannot resist the will of God, so we must simply be poor, abused little robots, right? Paul's answer is not satisfactory for most. Sadly, it is not satisfactory for many who name the name of Christ. Yet his answer is the only answer that can be given. "Who are you to answer back to God?" A good question. Will the creature say to the Creator, "Hey, why did you make me like this?" The potter has certain rights. He can make the pot in any way he desires. The pot can't complain, since the pot owes its existence to the potter. A pot that is used to catch rain-water from a leaky roof might rather be a fancy, painted pot on the dining room table— but it is not for the pot to say. The potter can make fancy pots, or plain old pots for everyday use. That is his right. He's the potter.

God is Creator. Sinful man denies this with every ounce of his being, but that does not change reality. God is our Creator. He made us. He made some for one purpose, others for another purpose. That is his right. He is the Creator. The Creator has certain rights. People can't complain, because people owe their existence to the Creator. A person who is used to bring about God's glory through their disobedience (like Pharaoh) can't complain, for that isn't their place.[21] The Creator can make people upon whom He will bestow mercy, and others for other purposes. He's the Creator.

A hard truth to accept? Yes, it is. But it is our duty to struggle with everything that God has revealed, even this. We must ask God to give us grace and mercy, and subdue our rebellious hearts. This is not something that anybody can argue you into believing, much less liking. That is God's work. I cannot force anyone to accept what this passage teaches. I cannot argue you into belief. And that is why I started out, at the beginning, with the challenge to accept what the Bible teaches, no matter how uncomfortable that might be. This passage is uncomfortable— of that there is no question. Thankfully though, truth is not determined by man's comfort level. Let's finish our survey with the following verses:

> *"What if God, choosing to show his wrath and make his power known, bore with great patience the objects of his wrath— prepared for destruction? What if he did this to make the riches of his glory known to the objects of his mercy, whom he prepared in advance for glory— even us, whom he also called, not only from the Jews but also from the Gentiles?"*
>
> —Romans 9:22-24

What if...? What if God did this? What if God desired to display the riches of his glory to those who are the objects of His mercy? Are we going to be so insolent, so foolish, to say that God's decision is wrong? Do we really think ourselves capable of standing before God, the pot before the Potter, to bring Him into judgment? What if? Do we have the right to question His wisdom?

What will you do? You cannot ignore this passage. It will be right there in Romans 9 every time you open your Bible. The issues are fundamental, basic, and yes, frightening. You may have to abandon long-held ways of thinking— thinking about yourself, thinking about God, thinking about your world. What will you do? Will you be like the woman who sat in my office one day, and when I expressed to her my acceptance of the teaching of this passage, said, "If that is what God is like, then I want nothing to do with Him"? Or will you ask God to open your eyes, and bring your heart into obedience? Only God's grace can enable you to do that— only He can plant such a desire in your heart. If that is your desire, you already knew that.

5

Was Anyone Saved at the Cross?

We say Christ so died that he infallibly secured the salvation of a multitude that no man can number, who through Christ's death not only may be saved, but are saved, must be saved, and cannot by any possibility run the hazard of being anything but saved.
— Charles Haddon Spurgeon

There was a time when I called myself a "4-Point Calvinist." There are many people who use this label and almost all the time the one point out of the five that they reject or cannot yet reconcile in their understanding is the dreaded "L" of Limited Atonement. There is just something about the concept that doesn't sit right with them. How can Christ's atonement be limited? And that is exactly what I asked until I began to seriously study the whole issue. It has been my experience that most who reject the *specific*, or *limited* atonement of Christ, do not *fully* grasp (believe?) the complete sovereignty of God, or one or more of the other four points. Most objections lodged against the doctrine of limited atonement are actually objections to one of the preceding points, not against limited atonement itself.

The "break" in my thinking came from reading Edwin Palmer's book, *The Five Points of Calvinism*[21]. While doing a radio program on the truth of God's electing grace, I was challenged by a caller regarding the death of Christ. He asked "Why would Christ die for the whole world if God did not intend to save everyone?" I looked at my co-host, and he looked at me, and I made a mental note to do more study into that particular question. I grabbed Palmer's book as soon as I returned home, and began to read the chapter on the atoning work of Christ.

I became a "full five-point Calvinist" upon reading the following section:

> The question that needs a precise answer is this: Did He or didn't He? Did Christ actually make a substitutionary sacrifice for sins or didn't He? If He did, then it was not for all the world, for then all the world would be saved.[22]

I was faced with a decision. If I maintained a "universal" atonement, that is, if I said that Christ died substitutionarily in the place of every single man and woman in all the world, then I was forced to either say that 1) everyone will be saved, or 2) the death of Christ is insufficient to save without additional works. I knew that I was not willing to believe that Christ's death could not save outside of human actions. So I had to understand that Christ's death was made in behalf of God's elect, and that it *does* accomplish its intention, it *does* save those for whom it is made.

At this point I realized that I had "limited" the atonement all along. In fact, if you do not believe in the Reformed doctrine of "limited atonement," you believe in a limited atonement anyway! How so? Unless you are a universalist (that is, unless you believe that everyone will be saved), then you believe that the atonement of Christ, if it is made for all men, is limited in its effect. You believe that Christ can die in someone's place and yet that person may still be lost for eternity. You limit the *power* and *effect* of the atonement. I limit the *scope* of the atonement, while saying that its power and effect is unlimited! One writer expressed it well when he said,

> Let there be no misunderstanding at this point. The Arminian limits the atonement as certainly as does the Calvinist. The Calvinist limits the extent of it in that he says it does not apply to all persons...while the Arminian limits the power of it, for he says

that in itself it does not actually save anybody. The Calvinist limits it quantitatively, but not qualitatively; the Arminian limits it qualitatively, but not quantitatively. For the Calvinist it is like a narrow bridge that goes all the way across the stream; for the Arminian it is like a great wide bridge that goes only half-way across. As a matter of fact, the Arminian places more severe limitations on the work of Christ than does the Calvinist.[23]

Therefore, we are not talking about presenting some terrible limitation on the work of Christ when we speak of "limited atonement." In fact, we are actually presenting a far *greater* view of the work of Christ on Calvary when we say that Christ's death actually *accomplishes* something in *reality* rather than only in *theory*. The atonement, we believe, was a real, actual, substitutionary one, not a possible, theoretical one that is dependent for its efficacy upon the actions of man. And, as one who often shares the gospel with people involved in false religious systems, I will say that the *Biblical* doctrine of the atonement of Christ is a powerful truth that is the *only* message that has real impact in dealing with the many heretical teachings about Christ that are present in our world today. Jesus Christ died in behalf of those that the Father had, from eternity, decreed to save. There is absolute unity between the Father and the Son in saving God's people. The Father decrees their salvation, the Son dies in their place, and the Spirit sanctifies them and conforms them to the image of Christ. This is the consistent testimony of Scripture.

The Intention of the Atonement

Why did Christ come to die? Did He come simply to make salvation *possible*, or did He come to actually *obtain eternal redemption* (Hebrews 9:12)? Let's consider some passages from Scripture in answer to this question.

> *"For the Son of Man came to seek and to save what was lost."* —Luke 19:10

Here the Lord Jesus Himself speaks of the reason for His

coming. He came to *seek* and to *save* the lost. Few have a problem with His seeking; many have a problem with the idea that He actually accomplished *all* of His mission. Jesus, however, made it clear that He came to actually *save* the lost. He did this by His death.

> "Here is a trustworthy saying that deserves full acceptance: Christ Jesus came into the world to save sinners—of whom I am the worst." —1 Timothy 1:15

Paul asserts that the purpose of Christ's coming into the world was to actually *save* sinners. Nothing in Paul's words leads us to the conclusion that is so popular today—that Christ's death simply makes salvation a *possibility* rather than a reality. Christ came to save. So, did He? And how did He? Was it not by His death? Most certainly. The atoning death of Christ provides forgiveness of sins for all those for whom it is made. That is why Christ came.

Christ's Intercessory Work

> "But because Jesus lives forever, he has a permanent priesthood. Therefore he is able to save completely those who come to God through him, because he always lives to intercede for them."   —Hebrews 7:24-26

The New Testament closely connects the work of Christ as our High Priest and intercessor with His death upon the cross. In this passage from Hebrews, we are told that the Lord Jesus, since He lives forever, has an unchangeable or permanent priesthood. He is not like the old priests who passed away, but is a perfect priest, because He remains forever. Because of this He is able to save *completely* those who come to God through Him. Why? Because He always lives to make intercession for them.

Now, before considering the relationship of the death of Christ to His intercession, I wish to emphasize the fact that the Bible says that *Christ is able to save men completely*. He is not limited simply to a secondary role as the great Assistor who makes it possible for man to save himself. Those who draw near to God through Christ will find full and complete salvation in Him. Furthermore, we must remember that Christ intercedes for those *who draw near to God*. I feel that it is obvious that Christ is not interceding for those who are not approaching God through Him. Christ's intercession is in behalf of the people of God. We shall see how important this is in a moment.

Upon what ground does Christ intercede before the Father? Does He stand before the Father and ask Him to forget His holiness, forget His justice, and simply pass over the sins of men? Of course not. The Son intercedes before the Father on the basis of His death. Christ's intercession is based upon the fact that He has died as the substitute for God's people, and, since He has borne their sins in His body on the tree (1 Peter 2:24), He can present His offering before the Father in their place, and intercede for them on this basis. The Son does not ask the Father to compromise His holiness, or to simply pass over sin. Christ took care of sin at Calvary, as we read—

> *"When Christ came as high priest of the good things that are already here, he went through the greater and more perfect tabernacle that is not man-made, that is to say, not a part of this creation. He did not enter by means of the blood of goats and calves; but he entered the Most Holy Place once for all by his own blood, having obtained eternal redemption."* —Hebrews 9:11-12

When Christ entered into the Holy of Holies, He did so "by his own blood." When He did this, we are told that He had "obtained eternal redemption." This again is not a *theoretical* statement, but a statement of fact. Christ did not enter into the Holy of Holies to *attempt* to gain redemption for His people! He entered in having already accomplished that. So what is He doing? Is His work of intercession *another* work alongside His sacrificial death? Is His death ineffective without this "other" work?

Christ's intercession is not a second work outside of His death. Rather, Christ is presenting before the Father His perfect and complete sacrifice. He is our High Priest, and the sacrifice He offers in our place is the sacrifice of Himself. He is our Advocate, as John said:

> My dear children, I write this to you so that you will not sin. But if anybody does sin, we have one who speaks to the Father in our defense—Jesus Christ, the Righteous One. He is the atoning sacrifice for our sins, and not only for ours but also for the sins of the whole world —1 John 2:1-2 [24]

Christ's atoning death is clearly connected with His advocacy before the Father. Therefore, we can see the following truths:

1) It is impossible that the Son would not intercede for everyone for whom He died. If Christ dies as their Substitute, how could He not present His sacrifice in their stead before the Father? Can we really believe that Christ would die for someone that He did not intend to save?

2) It is impossible that anyone for whom the Son did *not* die could receive Christ's intercession. If Christ did *not* die in behalf of a certain individual, how could Christ intercede for that individual, since He would have no grounds upon which to seek the Father's mercy?

3) It is impossible that anyone for whom the Son intercedes could be lost. Can we imagine the Son pleading before the Father, presenting His perfect atonement in behalf of an individual that He wishes to save, and the Father rejecting the Son's intercession? The Father always hears the Son (John 11:42). Would He not hear the Son's pleas in behalf of all that the Son desires to save? Furthermore, if we believe that Christ can intercede for someone that the Father will not save, then we must believe either (1) that there is dissension in the Godhead, the Father desiring one thing, the Son another, or (2) that the Father is *incapable* of doing what the Son desires Him to do. Both positions are utterly impossible.

That Christ does not act as High Priest for all men is clearly seen in His "High Priestly Prayer" in John 17. The Lord clearly distinguishes between the "world" and those who are His throughout the prayer, but verse 9 makes the point very strongly:

> *"I pray for them. I am not praying for the world, but for those you have given me, for they are yours."* —John 17:9

When Christ prays to the Father, He does not pray for the "world" but for those that have been given to Him by the Father (John 6:37).

For Whom Did Christ Die?

There are a number of Scriptures that teach us that the *scope* of Christ's death was limited to the elect. Here are just a few:

> *"Just as the Son of Man did not come to be served, but to serve, and to give his life as a ransom for many."*
> —Matthew 20:28

The "many" for whom Christ died are the elect of God, just as Isaiah had said long before,—

> *"By his knowledge my righteous servant will justify many, and he will bear their iniquities."*   —Isaiah 53:11

The Lord Jesus made it clear that His death was for His people when He spoke of the Shepherd and the sheep:

> *"I am the good shepherd. The good shepherd lays down his life for the sheep....just as the Father knows me and I know the Father—and I lay down my life for the sheep."*
> —John 10:11,15

The good Shepherd lays down His life in behalf of the sheep. Are all men the sheep of Christ? Certainly not, for most men do not know Christ, and Christ says that His sheep know Him (John 10:14). Further, Jesus specifically told the Jews who did not believe in Him, "but you do not believe because you are not my sheep" (John 10:26). Note that in contrast with the idea that we believe and therefore make ourselves Christ's sheep, Jesus says that they do not believe because they are not His sheep! Whether one is of Christ's sheep is the Father's decision (John 6:37, 8:47), not the sheep's!

> *"...just as Christ loved us and gave himself up for us as a*
> *fragrant offering and sacrifice to God....husbands, love your*
> *wives, just as Christ loved the church and gave himself up for*
> *her to make her holy, cleansing her by the washing with*
> *water through the word, and to present her to himself as a*
> *radiant church, without stain or wrinkle or any other*
> *blemish, but holy and blameless."*
>
> —*Ephesians 5:2, 25-27*

Christ gave Himself in behalf of His Church, His Body, and that for the purpose of cleansing her and making her holy. If this was His intention for the Church, why would He give Himself for those who are not of the Church? Would He not wish to make these "others" holy as well? Yet, if Christ died for all men, there are many, many who will remain impure for all eternity. Was Christ's death insufficient to cleanse them? Certainly not. Did He have a different goal in mind in dying for them?[25] No, His sacrificial death in behalf of His Church results in her purification, and this is what He intended for *all* for whom He died.

> *"He who did not spare His own Son, but gave him up for*
> *us all—how will he not also, along with him, graciously*
> *give us all things? Who will bring a charge against those*
> *whom God has chosen? It is God who justifies. Who is he*
> *that condemns? Christ Jesus, who died—more than that,*
> *who was raised to life—is at the right hand of God and*
> *is also interceding for us."*   —*Romans 8:32-34*

The Father gave the Son in our place. Who is the "our" of this passage? The text says that it is "those whom God has chosen," that is, the elect of God. Again, the intercessory work of Christ at the right hand of the Father is presented in perfect harmony with the death of Christ—those for whom Christ died are those for whom He intercedes. And, as this passage shows, if Christ intercedes for someone, who can possibly bring a charge against that person and hope to see them condemned? So we see what we have seen before: Christ dies in someone's place, He intercedes for them, and they are infallibly saved. Christ's work is complete and perfect. He is the powerful Savior, and He *never* fails to accomplish His purpose.

> *"Greater love has no one than this, that he lay down his life for his friends."* —John 15:13

Are all the friends of Christ? Do all own His name? Do all bow before Him and accept Him as Lord? Do all do His commandments (John 15:14)? Then not all are His friends.

> *"While we wait for the blessed hope— the glorious appearing of our great God and Savior, Jesus Christ, who gave himself for us to redeem us from all wickedness and to purify for himself a people that are his very own, eager to do what is good."* —Titus 2:13-14

Both the substitutionary element of the cross— gave *himself* for *us,* and its purpose— to redeem us and to purify, are forcefully presented to Titus. If it was the purpose of Christ to redeem and purify those for whom He died, can this possibly *not* take place?

> *"She will give birth to a son, and you are to give him the name Jesus, because he will save his people from their sins."* —Matthew 1:21

Christ *will* save *His people* from their sins. I ask what Edwin Palmer asked me before: Well, did He? Did He save His people, or did He not?

> *"I have been crucified with Christ and I no longer live, but Christ lives in me. The life I live in the body, I live by faith in the Son of God, who loved me and gave himself for me."* —Galatians 2:20

This is the common confession of every true believer in Christ. We died with Him, our Substitute, the one who loved us and gave Himself in our behalf.

We have seen, then, that the Word teaches that Christ died for many, for His sheep, for the Church, for the elect of God, for His friends, for a people zealous for good works, for His people, for each and every Christian.

Perfected and Sanctified

It is quite possible to fill entire volumes with a study of the atonement of Christ.[26] It is not our purpose to do so here. Instead, we shall close our brief survey of Scripture with these words—

> *"And by that will, we have been made holy through the sacrifice of the body of Jesus Christ once for all. Day after day every priest stands and performs his religious duties; again and again he offers the same sacrifice, which can never take away sins. But when this priest had offered for all time one sacrifice for sins, he sat down at the right hand of God. Since that time he waits for his enemies to be made his footstool, because by one sacrifice he has made perfect forever those who are being made holy."*
> —Hebrews 10:10-14

While we have seen many logical reasons for believing in limited atonement, and we have seen many references to Christ's death in behalf of His people, this one passage, above all others, to me, makes the doctrine a *must*. Listen closely to what we are told. First, what is the effect of the one time sacrifice of the body of Jesus Christ? What does verse 10 tell us? "We have been made holy," or, another translation would be, "We have been sanctified." The Greek language uses the perfect tense here, indicating a past, and completed, action. The death of Christ actually *makes us holy*. Do we believe this? Did the death of Christ actually sanctify those for whom it was made? Or did it simply make it possible for them to become holy? Again, these are questions that cannot be easily dismissed. The writer goes on to describe how this priest, Jesus, sat down at the right hand of God, unlike the old priests who had to keep performing sacrifices over and over and over again. His work, on the contrary, is perfect and complete. He can rest, for by His one sacrifice He has *made perfect* those who are experiencing the sanctifying work of the Spirit in their lives. He made them perfect, complete. The term refers to a completion, a finishing. Again, do we believe that Christ's death does this? And, if we see the plain teaching of Scripture, are we willing to alter our beliefs, and our methods of proclaiming the gospel, to fit the truth?

What about Faith?

One common belief needs to be addressed in passing. Many who believe in a "universal" or non-specific atonement, assert that while Christ died for all, His atonement is only effective for those who believe. We shall discuss the fact that faith itself is the gift of God, given only to the elect of God, in the next chapter. But for now, we defer to the great Puritan writer, John Owen, in answering this question:

> To which I may add this dilemma to our Universalists:—God imposed his wrath due unto, and Christ underwent the pains of hell for, either all the sins of all men, or all the sins of some men, or some sins of all men. If the last, some sins of all men, then have all men some sins to answer for, and so shall no man be saved; for if God enter into judgment with us, though it were with all mankind for one sin, no flesh should be justified in his sight: "If the LORD should mark iniquities, who should stand?" Ps. 130:3... If the second, that is it which we affirm, that Christ in their stead and room suffered for all the sins of all the elect in the world. If the first, why, then are not all freed from the punishment of all their sins? You will say, "Because of their unbelief; they will not believe." But this unbelief, is it a sin, or not? If not, why should they be punished for it? If it be, then Christ underwent the punishment due to it, or not. If so, then why must that hinder them more than their other sins for which he died from partaking of the fruit of his death? If he did not, then he did not die for all their sins. Let them choose which part they will.[27]

Conclusion

Some object to the doctrine of limited atonement on very pragmatic grounds. "The doctrine destroys evangelism, because you cannot tell people that Christ died for them, because you don't know!" Yet, we ask, is there an advantage in presenting to men an atonement that is theoretical, a Savior whose work is incomplete, and a gospel that is but a possibility? What kind of proclamation will God honor with His Spirit: one that is tailored to seek "success," or one that is bound to the truth of the Word of God? When the Apostles preached the Gospel, they did not say, "Christ died for all men everywhere, and it is up to you to make His work effective." They taught that Christ died for sinners, and that it was the duty of every man to repent and believe. They knew that only God's grace could bring about repentance and faith in the human heart. And far from that being a *hindrance* to their evangelistic work, it was the power behind it! They proclaimed a *powerful* Savior, whose work is all sufficient, and who saves men totally and completely! They knew that God was about bringing men to Himself, and, since He is the sovereign of the universe, there is no power on earth that will stay His hand! Now *there* is a solid basis for evangelism! And what could be more of a comfort to the heart that is racked with guilt than to know that Christ has died for sinners, and that His work is not just theoretical, but is *real*?

The Church needs to challenge the world again with the daring proclamation of a gospel that is offensive—offensive because it speaks of God saving those whom He will, offensive because it proclaims a sovereign Savior who redeems *His people*.

6

A Dead Man's Tale

No more soul-destroying doctrine could well be devised than the doctrine that sinners can regenerate themselves, and repent and believe just when they please....As it is a truth both of Scripture and of experience that the unrenewed man can do nothing of himself to secure his salvation, it is essential that he should be brought to a practical conviction of that truth. When thus convinced, and not before, he seeks help from the only source whence it can be obtained. — Charles Hodge

The doctrines of grace flow naturally from one to another. That is not because they are built upon the "wisdom of man," but because they reflect the perfect consistency of the Word of God. The doctrine of "irresistible grace" flows naturally and logically from what has come before. If God is all sovereign, if man is dead in sin and incapable of saving himself, if God has eternally elected to save certain men and women, and if Christ has died in their place, then it is obvious that God's eternal plan will not fall on its face when it comes time for the individual to enter into the salvation that was secured for him in eternity past. When God decrees that one of the elect is to be regenerated and enter into spiritual life, this will take place, infallibly, without question. This is what "irresistible grace" means. Quite simply, the doctrine affirms that (1) God's grace is powerful and completely able to accomplish that which He intends (which is why some prefer the name "effective grace"), and (2) man, being dead in sin, is incapable of resisting God's grace that brings regeneration.

This doctrine is very important in evaluating much modern preaching. How often do we hear the gospel presented as if man had the ability, by believing, to save himself? How often do we hear, "You must repent, and then believe in Jesus, and then you will be born again." But this is not what the Bible teaches, no matter how often we may hear it repeated! Let's look to the Word of God as our guide.

The Lord Jesus on the New Birth

"In reply Jesus declared, 'I tell you the truth, no one can see the kingdom of God unless he is born again.' " —John 3:3

The interview between Nicodemus and Jesus Christ is probably the most famous of all private conversations. Yet a fundamental teaching of this passage is often missed in our day. When speaking of the kingdom of God, Jesus taught Nicodemus that to even see the kingdom, one had to be born again. Being born again precedes seeing the kingdom of God. If one cannot even see the kingdom of God without first being born again, how can one "decide" to enter into it? Nicodemus is surprised at this, and Jesus goes on to explain Himself:

"Jesus answered, 'I tell you the truth, no one can enter the kingdom of God unless he is born of water and the Spirit. Flesh gives birth to flesh, but the Spirit gives birth to spirit. You should not be surprised at my saying, "You must be born again." ' "   —John 3:5-7

Being born of water and Spirit must be understood in the light of the words of Ezekiel 36:25-27 and Titus 3:5-7, both of which inform us that "water" refers to the cleansing work of God by His Spirit. The words of Christ inform us that we are in need of a spiritual birth. This is perfectly in line with what Paul taught about our spiritual deadness. We must be changed— reborn— before we can enter into the kingdom of God. But this spiritual birth does not come as the result of human actions, but must precede those actions. Babies do not "cause" themselves to be born by doing this or that; babies do what babies do because they have been born. These are basic truths, and we must be consistent in applying them to our understanding of the message of Christ, for Christ was certainly consistent in teaching them!

> "For just as the Father raises the dead and gives them life, even so the Son gives life to whom he is pleased to give it."
> —John 5:21

The Father and the Son are united in giving life to the dead. Who are these dead who receive life from the Father? Clearly, they are the same ones who are given by the Father to the Son (John 6:37) and to whom the Son reveals the Father (Matthew 11:27), that is, the elect of God. This gift of life is a gift of grace. There surely is no thought here (or anywhere in Scripture) that the Father or the Son simply *attempt* to raise the dead, nor should anyone dare to think that having attempted, that either the Father or the Son could fail to raise someone to life! Those who are dead, obviously, are not able to stop God from raising them to life!

The *efficiency* or *irresistibility* of God's sovereign grace is presented with force by the Lord Jesus in John 6:37 and 45:

> All that the Father gives me will come to me, and whoever comes to me I will never drive away....It is written in the Prophets: "They will all be taught by God." Everyone who listens to the Father and learns from him comes to me, and I will raise him up at the last day.   —John 6:45

There is no doubt that Jesus believed that all who were given to Him by the Father would come to Him. Everyone who listens to the Father and learns from Him will, infallibly, come to Christ, and will therefore be raised up at the last day. When God's grace enters into their lives, and they are born again, regenerated, drawn— whichever of the many terms the Bible uses to describe the work of regeneration— the recipient of that grace will be changed forever. It is simply impossible that God can fail when He moves to bring one of the elect to life. *Whether* we become born again is not a matter of *if* we decide to, but is the result of *the sovereign action of God, and always results* in our coming to Christ. First we are regenerated,— then we believe!

By Him You are in Christ...

The Church has experienced the fact of God's effective grace in her missionary work. When Paul and his missionary band entered into Philippi, they encountered a woman named Lydia upon the banks of the river. The Scriptures tell us,

> *"One of those listening was a woman named Lydia, a*
> *dealer in purple cloth from the city of Thyatira, who was*
> *a worshiper of God. The Lord opened her heart to respond*
> *to Paul's message."*   —Acts 16:14

Lydia was a worshiper of God. Yet we are told that she was still dependent upon the work of the Spirit of God in her heart, for the Lord "opened" her heart to respond to Paul's preaching. Every person must have this take place in their life if they are to be saved. God can open hearts, and this is the tremendous truth that empowers the Church's witness. Indeed, without the promise that God can save anyone He desires to save, we would have little promise of the success of our work. God's power is the foundation of the Church's missions work, and when we face the hatred of the world, we know that our God is in charge, and there is no power in heaven or in earth that can stop Him from accomplishing the salvation of His elect. Paul told Timothy—

> *"Therefore I endure everything for the sake of the elect,*
> *that they may obtain the salvation that is in Christ Jesus,*
> *with eternal glory."*   —2 Timothy 2:10

Given what Paul suffered in his life, we can see the *strength* and *commitment* that comes from understanding God's elective and powerful grace! Lydia certainly knew the truth—

> *"It is because of him that you are in Christ Jesus, who has become for us wisdom from God— that is, our righteousness, holiness and redemption. Therefore, as it is written: "Let him who boasts boast in the Lord."*
> —*1 Corinthians 1:30- 31*

"It is *because of him* that you are in Christ Jesus." It was not, as we see over and over again, that God simply made an offer, and we made the final, operative decision. The Greek literally means, "it is *from Him* you are in Christ Jesus...." God is the instrument, the means by which we are in Christ. Nowhere does Paul say that it was our final decision, our action that placed us in Christ Jesus. God acts with a particular purpose, and we respond to His mighty power. The writer of these words, Paul, had experienced God's mighty grace personally. As he told the Galatians,

> *"But when God, who set me apart from birth and called me by his grace, was pleased to reveal his Son in me so that I might preach him among the Gentiles..."* —*Galatians 1:15*

The timing of Paul's conversion was God's, not Paul's. Certainly, in Paul's case, God's prominent role in bringing about his salvation was more visible than for most of us. Few of us have been knocked to the ground by bright lights, followed by the voice of the Lord. But the fact that it is God who saves— when and where God wills to do so— is consistent in the salvation of all of God's people. God chose to reveal His Son in Paul at the point in time that was in accordance with His will, not Paul's. God was not reacting to some good deed on Paul's part when He brought Paul to salvation. As Paul told Titus,

> *"He saved us, not because of righteous things we had done, but because of his mercy. He saved us through the washing of rebirth and renewal by the Holy Spirit."* —*Titus 3:5*

God's mercy brought about our salvation, not any action on our part, and that includes faith! We cannot force God to save us by believing in Him (even if we could believe in Him outside of His grace, which we cannot). We are saved, not by first doing a series of things like believing, repenting, reforming our lives, but by the washing of regeneration and the renewal of the Holy Spirit— both actions of God.[28]

Regeneration—Then Faith

Everyone who believes that Jesus is the Christ is born of God, and everyone who loves the father loves his child as well."   —1 John 5:1

Do we first believe so that we can be born again, or do we believe *because* we have been born again? John taught the latter in his first epistle. A more literal translation of the Greek would be, "Everyone believing (present tense) that Jesus is the Christ has been born of God (perfect tense). The belief is an on-going thing; being born of God is a completed action in the past. Being born of God occurs *before* the believing, and, in fact, is the basis of belief (faith). Those who are born of God believe that Jesus is the Christ. In a very similar passage earlier in the epistle, John taught the same thing:

If you know that he is righteous, you know that everyone who does what is right has been born of him." —1 John 2:29

The grammar in this passage is the same as that in 5:1. The one who is doing righteousness ("does what is right") has been born of God. We do not do righteousness so that we can be born again; we do righteousness because we have already been born again. The new birth changes us and it then becomes our nature, as new creations in Christ Jesus (1 Corinthians 5:17), to believe, to repent, to do good works, to do righteousness.

The idea that faith and repentance follow God's work of regeneration is not the majority opinion in most churches today. But the Bible is clear on the topic, and what is more, the Scriptures are equally clear in proclaiming that we are dependent upon God for the ability to believe, and to repent.

The Gifts of Faith and Repentance

Can just anyone believe and be saved? Such a question has two answers. First, we know that man is incapable of coming to Christ outside of the Father's drawing (John 6:44), and that no man seeks after God (Romans 3:11). Secondly, what are we talking about when we speak of "faith"? What is true, saving faith? The Bible speaks often of the absolute necessity of believing on Jesus Christ and repenting of our sins. Yet the Bible also shows us that we are incapable of doing those very things! How are we to understand this?

When we looked at man's *inabilities*, we noted the principle that if we find the Bible exhorting us to ask something of God, we should realize that we must lack that which we are told to seek from Him. Further, if we are to give thanks to God for something, we again should realize that it must come from His hand, and that we are dependent upon Him for that thing. With these thoughts in mind, let us note the Biblical view of true, saving faith.

> *"We always thank God, the Father of our Lord Jesus Christ, when we pray for you, because we have heard of your faith in Christ Jesus and of the love you have for all the saints."*
> —*Colossians 1:3-4*

This kind of greeting is to be found in most of the Apostle's letters. He gives thanks for the Colossians on two accounts; one, because of their faith, and two, because of their love. Why would Paul give thanks to God for the Colossians' faith and love? Quite simply because faith and love are works of the Spirit of God in the heart of the redeemed. Exactly the same truth can be found in 2 Thessalonians 1:3, where again we find Paul thanking God for the faith of believers. If we thank God for something, it must come from His hand.

When Peter healed the man at the gate of the Temple, what did he say about the man's faith?

"By faith in the name of Jesus, this man whom you see and know was made strong. It is Jesus' name and the faith that comes through him that has given this complete healing to him, as you can all see."   —Acts 3:16

Where did the man's faith come from? It came through Christ. It was not his to do with as he pleased, but it was the gift of God to him. True, saving faith, in contrast to dead, useless, one-time, flash-in-the-pan faith, comes through Christ. He is the "author and finisher" of that kind of faith (Hebrews 12:2). That is, He is the one who starts, begins, and is the source of faith, and He is the one who completes, finishes, perfects faith. He is the beginning and the end of faith, and the object of faith as well! Peter had not changed his beliefs many years later when he wrote:

"Through him you believe in God, who raised him from the dead and glorified him, and so your faith and hope are in God."   —1 Peter 1:21

It is through Christ that we have faith, it is through Christ that we believe in God. Peter was not the only Apostle to teach this!

"For it has been granted to you on behalf of Christ not only to believe on him, but also to suffer for him."
—Philippians 1:29

What has been granted to believers? Yes, surely, to suffer for Christ is part of God's will for the Church. But don't speed past the first statement to get to the second. It is taken for granted that the Christians knew that it had been granted to them to believe in Christ! If it had to be granted to them, then obviously it is only within the power of God to give true, saving faith, just as it is only within His power to give us the right and proper kind of love that we are to have for Him and for one another.

"Peace to the brothers, and love with faith from God the Father and the Lord Jesus Christ. Grace to all who love our Lord Jesus Christ with an undying love."
—Ephesians 6:23-24

A common element of Paul's writings is the connection of the terms grace, peace, and love. A quick glance at such passages as Philippians 1:2 or Ephesians 1:2 will bear this statement out. Few would argue that we should ask God to help us to love Him properly. This kind of love comes from God, and is supernatural in origin. In the same way, peace and grace also flow from God to the believer. But here in Ephesians 6 another element is present: faith. If grace must come from God, and if peace must come from God, and if love must come from God, then faith, too, must come from God, even as all the rest. If we must have the Spirit to have real peace, true grace, and undying love, how can we have saving faith in any other way? And did not Paul directly teach that faith is a work of the Spirit?

> *"But the fruit of the Spirit is love, joy, peace, patience, kindness, goodness, faithfulness, gentleness and self-control. Against such things there is no law." —Galatians 5:22*

The term translated "faithfulness" is actually simply the word "faith." This is the fruit of the Spirit of God in the life of the believer. It is a gift of grace, and it is outside of the capacity of the natural man.

One of the most common passages that is presented in this context is Ephesians 2:8-9. It is such a well-known section that it is almost in danger of being ignored due to familiarity—

> *"For it is by grace you have been saved, through faith— and this not from yourselves, it is the gift of God— not by works, so that no one can boast."*

For our present purposes, we point out that the entire initial clause, including grace, salvation, *and faith*, is summed up in "and *this* not of yourselves," Grace does not come from man, it is the gift of God. Salvation does not come from man, it is the gift of God. Therefore, faith does not come from man. It, too, is the gift of God. We are the *recipients* of God's grace, and we are the *recipients* of His gift of faith, just as Peter taught,—

> *"Simon Peter, a servant and apostle of Jesus Christ, to those*

who through the righteousness of our God and Savior Jesus
Christ have received a faith as precious as ours."
                                                    —2 Peter 1:1

Saving faith is a precious gift from God, given to us in Christ
Jesus.[29] How often do we thank Him for our faith?

But we mentioned *both* faith and repentance as gifts. What
evidence is there that repentance comes from God as well? We
have already seen some evidence of this. When we spoke of the
captivity of man in sin, we referenced 2 Timothy 2:24-25, which
spoke of God "granting" to men repentance so that they could
escape from the snare of the devil. If men could repent at their
leisure, why would God have to "grant" them repentance? And
does not Paul teach us that it is the kindness of God that leads
us to repentance (Romans 2:4)?

Paul's doctrine of the inability of man provides us with our
firmest testimony, however. In Romans 8:5-9, Paul contrasts the
"fleshly" man, that is, the unregenerate man, with the spiritual
man, that is, the one who has been made spiritually alive in
Christ. We read,—

> *"For those who are according to the flesh mind the things*
> *of the flesh, but those who are according to the Spirit mind*
> *the things of the Spirit. For the mind set on the flesh is*
> *death, but the mind set on the Spirit is life and peace, for*
> *the mind set on the flesh is hostile toward God, for it is not*
> *subject to the law of God, neither is it even able to do so,*
> *and those who are in the flesh are unable to please God."*
> *   —Romans 8:5-8* [30]

Those who are "in the flesh" are hostile to God. Their minds
are at enmity with God. They are not subject to the law of God,
neither indeed are they capable of submitting themselves to
God's law. Put simply, they are absolutely incapable of doing
what is pleasing in God's sight. This is in perfect harmony with
what we saw in our previous examination of total depravity. So
here is our question: *Is repentance pleasing to God?* Obviously,
it is. So, can the "fleshly" man repent, and do what is pleasing

to God? Not if Paul meant what he said in Romans 8:8. Therefore, the one who repents must be the one who has been made alive by the Spirit of God, so that he can then do what is pleasing to God, including both to believe, and to repent.

When God raises up one of His elect to spiritual life, He gives to that person certain gifts. He gives that person faith— abiding faith, faith that is centered on Jesus Christ and Him alone. He gives a faith that will endure, and faith that will persevere unto the end. This faith is *supernatural— powerful— lasting— complete*. Peter does indeed say that we are kept by the power of God "through faith" (1 Peter 1:5). But the faith of which he speaks is the faith that is ours from Christ. It is faith that has Jesus as its author and finisher. It is faith that lasts, it is faith that is part of God's creating a new creature in Christ Jesus. Another gift that is given is repentance. The believer, because he has been changed, because he has been made new, hates his sin. He knows that his sin offends the holy God, and he wishes to flee from sin. He prays to hate sin, and to live a holy life. This is the natural desire of the changed person. God enables him to repent, to turn from his sin.

God does not just "partially" save someone. Regeneration is radical. God goes all the way in His work, and He will *never* fail to do exactly what His will demands. When God's grace moves into someone's life, they *will be changed*. There is no possibility of frustration, no possibility of failure. God's sovereign grace will accomplish *all* of His holy will.

7

Secure in The Father and The Son

"Christ is to be answerable for all those that are given to Him, at the last day, and therefore we need not doubt but that He will certainly employ all the power of His Godhead to secure and save all those that He must be accountable for." — Thomas Brooks

Few debates have generated more heat than the one that surrounds the concept of the "perseverance of the saints" or "eternal security." There are very few Christians who have not had to come down on one side of the issue or the other. Yet many, many of the debates on the subject of the perseverance of the saints have taken place without the proper foundation, in fact, without any foundation at all. It seems rather obvious that one cannot possibly address the issue of eternal security without *first* addressing the issues that have made up the bulk of the preceding material. How can one decide if salvation is eternal if one has not first discussed the role of God and man in salvation, the nature of God's dealings with men, and the abilities (or lack thereof) of man outside of God's Spirit? Surely what one believes about these things will be *determinative* in the discussion of eternal security (or the opposite position, as I like to call it, "eternal insecurity").

Few issues, however, focus our attention upon the central truths of the gospel as this one. To discuss the perseverance of the saints is to decide whether one believes in a *man-centered* gospel, where man is the primary decision maker, or a *God-centered* gospel, where God is the gracious sovereign who has the power to accomplish salvation. If the gospel is but a plan and not a reality, and if man's decision is final, then obviously the entire concept of eternal security has no foundation. If I decided to get into this arrangement, I can decide to get out of it as well. Or, if my continuing in salvation is dependent upon my works, upon my effort, and if God has not guaranteed His work in my life, then I will find some way to mess everything up and lose even that offer of eternal life. If what has come before is not true, then there simply is no reason to believe that I will persevere in faith.

If what has come before however, accurately presents the truth of the inspired Scriptures, then it is easy to see how the perseverance of the saints is simply the only possible conclusion to the completed, perfect, and finished work of Jesus Christ. If God has eternally set His love upon the elect, and if in eternity past He chose them in Christ Jesus, united them with Christ, sent His Son to die in their place, raised them up with Christ, and has placed His Almighty Spirit in them to accomplish His desire, how could it possibly happen that they be lost? Could God truly decree their salvation, and yet be frustrated in His desires? Surely not. Everything we have seen militates against such a thought. Further, if Jesus Christ has died in their place, upon what possible basis could they be condemned? Jesus Christ took their place, and bore their sins. How could they then be lost? Christ did not just bear *some* of their sins, but *all* of their sins. We have already seen the impossibility of the idea that one for whom Christ died, for whom He pleads before the Father, could possibly be lost. The perseverance of the saints, then, flows *necessarily* from the God-centered gospel of the Bible.

What this does not mean, of course, is that we can then ignore presenting Biblical evidence for the belief, for it is incumbent upon us to do so. However, it does point out what was said before. Without the foundation of God's electing grace and His almighty sovereignty, we are left arguing one "set" of Scriptures against another, one set teaching eternal security, the other supposedly teaching the possibility of losing one's salvation. However, once the sovereignty of God and the deadness of man in sin has been established, it becomes obvious that those passages that are normally used to deny eternal security cannot possibly be interpreted in that way, for to do such is to compromise the most basic elements of the revelation of God and His purposes in this world.

The reader may have noted at this point that I am using two different terms to describe this one doctrine, "eternal security" and "the perseverance of the saints." Others throw in a third, "the preservation of the saints." The first term is very common, the second is the most accurate, and the third has some important truths to communicate as well. Eternal security, unfortunately, often communicates the thought of "once saved, always saved." While we will affirm that if a person is truly born again by the Spirit of God that they can never be lost, viewing the doctrine in this way is but a part of the whole. Many have abused the term, using it as an excuse for cold, unholy living. As we shall emphasize, the doctrine in no way gives comfort to those who do not care about the state of their soul. The doctrine takes for granted the reality of a living, true, supernatural faith. Indeed, that is why the term "perseverance of the saints" is probably the most accurate description of the doctrine. This speaks more directly to the real meaning of this truth, for it says that God has done something in the life of the believer that changes him and results in his *perseverance* in faith. It tells us that there is a living, continuing faith present in the life of the believer, a faith that will not ultimately fail, but will endure to the end. God is working in our lives, and He will accomplish His purpose of conforming us to the image of His Son. Because this is true, we will persevere in faith toward God. But the third phrase, the preservation of the saints, helps us to balance our thinking, for the power by which we persevere is God's power, not our own. We are saved by grace, and we are kept by the power of grace as well. God will preserve us by making us to persevere. Our faith, being a gift from God, will last, simply because it is God's will that it do so. He will uphold us with His right hand.

I shall begin the Biblical survey of this doctrine with the one passage that I believe to be the most obvious, the most inarguable presentation of the absolute security of the elect in Christ Jesus, John 6:37-39.

The Father's Will for the Son

"All that the Father gives me will come to me, and whoever comes to me I will never drive away. For I have come down from heaven not to do my will but to do the will of him who sent me. And this is the will of him who sent me, that I shall lose none of all that he has given me, but raise them up at the last day."

We have already seen John 6:37 in the discussions of election ("the Father gives") and effectual grace ("will come"), and now we meet this passage again with reference to the perseverance of the saints. The Lord Jesus gives us His word that He would never, ever drive away one who has come to Him in faith. The language of the text contains the strongest possible denial of the possibility that the Lord would ever cast out one who trusts in Him for salvation. At the same time, throughout this passage, the original language informs us that the one who "comes" to Christ is the one who is constantly *coming* to Christ. That is, the Lord is not here talking about people who simply tip their hat in God's direction and hope for the best. He is talking about people who are *coming* to Christ. He is the center of their faith. Their faith is on-going, deep, alive, vital. It is saving faith. Nowhere in this passage (or anywhere in the Word of God) will we find a promise of security for those who simply give lip-service to God, but whose hearts are far removed from Him. No one who has simply "walked an aisle" and shaken someone's hand, or who has gone through various rituals or ceremonies, but whose heart does not long for Christ, can claim these promises as his own. These words are for the elect of God, in whom God instills living, saving faith by His Spirit. It is this one who can rest, knowing that His Lord will ever be gracious toward Him. Christ will never cast him out.

This would be enough for anyone, but in His graciousness, the Lord has given us even more. He reveals to us yet another tremendous truth, one that is often missed when we speak of the truth of the perseverance of the saints. He speaks of the fact that He has come into the world to do the will of the Father. We know that the Son is perfectly obedient to the Father, so there is no question that He will do exactly what the Father desires. And, further, we know that the Son has all authority in heaven and in earth, and is therefore capable of doing all that the Father assigns to Him. So what does the Father ask the Son to do? What is the Father's will? "That I shall lose none of all that he has given me, but raise them up at the last day." Take time to seriously consider what is said here.

The Father's will for the Son involves two aspects, the first negative, the second positive. First, the Son is not to lose any of those that have been given to Him by the Father. God the Father, in His electing grace, has given men to the Son. It is His will that the Son should not lose any of those who are so given. Secondly, the Son is charged with their salvation, for He is to raise them up at the last day. In other words, the Son is to bring about the full salvation of all of God's people. He is to keep them, and He is to provide for their resurrection at the last day.

So I ask a simple question of anyone who would consider denying the eternal security of the saints: Is it possible that the Son of God will *fail* to do the will of the Father? I realize that the vast majority of those who deny eternal security are not *pur-*

posefully attempting to cast doubt upon the ability, or obedience, of the Savior. However, that does not change the fact that, if we say that one can be truly saved, and then lost,[31] we are saying that Christ can fail in doing the will of the Father.

This "failure" could take two forms. First, Christ could simply disobey the Father. Second, Christ could be found insufficient to the task, and therefore fail due to weakness. Can the Christian heart even begin to consider either of these two possibilities? Of course not! Christ always does what pleases the Father, and He is the mighty Son of God, the one who created all things and holds the universe together (Colossians 1:16-17)! It is utterly impossible that He could be thwarted in His work. Therefore, it is equally impossible that any of those who have been given by the Father to the Son could be lost.

Many of the same themes are to be found in the tenth chapter of the Gospel of John. Again, God's people, the elect, His sheep, are in view, and the complete unity of the Father and Son in bringing about their salvation is being presented. We read,

> *"But you do not believe because you are not my sheep. My sheep listen to my voice; I know them, and they follow me. I give them eternal life, and they shall never perish; no one can snatch them out of my hand. My Father, who has given them to me, is greater than all; no one can snatch them out of my Father's hand. I and the Father are one."*
> —John 10:26-30

Christ's sheep listen to His voice, and they follow Him. Who are His sheep? They are those that the Father has given to Him. God is the one who decides who is a sheep and who is not. When one is a sheep, one knows Christ, and one follows Him. Again, the fact that we are talking about a living faith, a true disciple, must be emphasized. Those who have eternal life as a gift from Christ are those who hear His voice and follow Him. They are not simply surface followers, easy-believers. They follow their Shepherd. These are the ones of whom the Lord says, "no one can snatch them out of my hand." They are secure in the hands of the one who formed eternity itself. And if that were not enough, the Lord finishes by affirming the commitment of the Father to the salvation of the elect as well, resulting in that great statement of the unity of the Father and the Son being one in their work of bringing men to salvation.[32]

The Lord Jesus spoke of giving eternal life to His sheep. In John 5:24, He spoke of the same precious gift:

> *"I tell you the truth, whoever hears my word and believes him who sent me has eternal life and will not be condemned; he has crossed over from death to life."*

The believer *has*, present tense, right now, eternal life. He will not be condemned, but has *already* crossed over from death to life. How can one who already *has* eternal life, who cannot be condemned, and who has already crossed over to life, be lost? How can he die and be condemned? Such a scenario is no more possible than the idea that Christ could fail to do the will of the Father, or that the Father would fail to answer the prayer of the Son recorded in John 17:11-12,15:

> *"Holy Father, protect them by the power of your name— the name you gave me— so that they may be one as we are one. While I was with them, I protected them and kept them safe by that name you gave me. None has been lost except the one doomed to destruction so that Scripture would be fulfilled...My prayer is not that you take them out of the world but that you protect them from the evil one.*

Such words, when heard against the backdrop of the awesome sovereignty of God that we studied earlier, carry tremendous meaning for the believer. The Son asks the Father to protect His people. Since we know that the Father is not limited in His power by the creature man, and since we know that He will do whatever pleases Him, then it is obvious that the Father will grant the request of the Son, and will protect His people. They are secure, they will persevere in the faith.

When the Lord Jesus stands as judge in the last day, and many ungodly men stand before Him and plead that they had professed faith in His name, and had done great deeds in His name, He will say to them,—

"I never knew you. Away from me, you evildoers."
—Matthew 7:23

Those words, "I never knew you," will echo throughout eternity in the ears of those who played at religion, but never dealt with Jesus Christ, never *came* to Him in faith. For argument sake though, let us for a moment forget everything that has come before and assume it is possible for a person to lose their salvation. Let us assume that some of those who stand before Christ had, at one time, been of His sheep. Do we remember what Jesus said at John 10:14? "I am the good shepherd; I know my sheep and my sheep know me." The good Shepherd *knows* His sheep. There is intimate, personal knowledge between the Lord and His people.

When we compare the words of the Lord in Matthew 7:23 with His statement in John 10:14, we immediately see the problem with the entire idea that one of Christ's sheep can be lost. When Christ expels the evildoers in Matthew 7, He does so with the words "I never knew you." Yet He also teaches that He *knows* His sheep. How, then, could one of Christ's sheep ever stand before Him and hear the words, "I *never* knew you"? Christ could not say this in truth to one who had once been saved. He would have to say, "I *once* knew you, but I do not any longer." But this is not what He says. Therefore, the idea that one of Christ's sheep could be lost is contradictory to the Scriptural witness.

Before moving on to Paul's witness to the eternal security of the believer, I wish to note the *centrality* of Christ in this issue. We have noted that He is the "author and finisher" of our faith (Hebrews 12:2). If the Lord is the one who starts our faith, and if He is the one who finishes, completes, and perfects our faith, how can we possibly say that our faith may "fail"? Surely this highlights the importance of recognizing the supernatural origin of true, saving faith. If faith is simply something that lies within us, that we muster and exercise outside of the enabling power of God, then the possibility of its failure, and hence our being lost, is understandable. But the Bible does not present faith in this way. Faith is created by the Lord Jesus, it finds its object in its Creator, and will be finished by Him as well. From beginning to end, the Lord Jesus is Savior in the fullest possible sense. Therefore, if we claim that we can lose our faith, and hence be lost, are we not, *again*, laying the true blame at the feet of Jesus Christ? When we confess the truth of the doctrine of the perseverance of the saints, we are doing nothing more than saying that Jesus Christ is the *perfect* Savior.

The Confident Apostle

"Being confident of this, that he who began a good work in you will carry it on to completion until the day of Christ Jesus."   —Philippians 1:6

The Apostle Paul expressed confidence in the salvation of the believers at Philippi. But his confidence was not in the Philippians themselves. His reason for trusting that they would inherit eternal glory was not because they were so good, or so wonderful, or so strong in doing good works. No, his confidence was in the God who had begun a good work in their midst. His confidence was in the promises and purpose of God. God had begun the work, and God would complete the work.

It is quite simply impossible to make heads or tails of Paul's theology without recognizing his total acceptance of the sovereign character of the grace of God. As the Reformers often said, they were not "creating" anything new in their theology. Paul had taught everything they were teaching long, long before. Paul was, quite simply, a Calvinist, only because Calvin followed Paul's teaching so closely. Paul believed in the sovereignty of God, the total depravity of man, the unconditional, sovereign election of God, the perfect, substitutionary, and finished work of Christ, the effectual, powerful grace of God, and the truth of the security of those who were the objects of God's grace. These truths flow in and out of his words, finding expression in a number of ways, only a few of which appear in what follows.

> *"Therefore, since we have been justified through faith,*
> *we have peace with God through our Lord Jesus Christ."*
> *—Romans 5:1*

Paul taught the doctrine of justification by faith, not by works. We are made right with God not by anything we can do or have done, but simply by His mercy and grace. We believe in Christ, and on the basis of that faith, God declares us righteous in His sight. This righteousness is perfect and complete, lacking nothing, and because of this we *have* peace with God.

The peace of which Paul speaks is a perfect peace. It reflects the Hebrew understanding of *shalom*. This kind of peace is not simply a lack of hostilities. The term would not describe a situation in which you had two opposing armies poised to do battle, yet no fighting was yet taking place. That is not peace. Shalom speaks of wellness, of goodness. This kind of peace is a positive peace. And this is the kind of peace we have with God through Jesus Christ.

Yet, if it is possible for us to fall from our position, to be lost for eternity through some action of our own, how can we say that we truly have peace with God? If our relationship with God can again erupt into full scale war, and if we can again become enemies of God (Romans 8:7), how can this be called "peace"? No, the peace we have through Jesus Christ is not simply a "cease-fire" but a true peace, based upon His completed and finished work in our behalf. It is the peace of security in Him. It is the peace of knowing the truth of these words:

> *"Therefore, there is now no condemnation for those who are*
> *in Christ Jesus." —Romans 8:1*

The one who is "in Christ" does not know condemnation. Christ has been condemned, and has died, in his place. He no longer fears condemnation because he knows the all-sufficient

Savior. Can the one who denies eternal security say this? Not with honesty. As long as anyone's view of the gospel remains man-centered rather than God-centered, these passages present empty promises, quaint hopes, but not divine realities. How can the following words have meaning outside of an understanding of God's sovereign grace?

> "What, then, shall we say in response to this? If God is for us, who can be against us? He who did not spare his own Son, but gave him up for us all— how will he not also, along with him, graciously give us all things? Who will bring a charge against those whom God has chosen? It is God who justifies. Who is he that condemns? Christ Jesus, who died— more than that, who was raised to life— is at the right hand of God and is also interceding for us. Who shall separate us from the love of Christ? Shall trouble or hardship or persecution or famine or nakedness or danger or sword?... For I am convinced that neither death nor life, neither angels nor demons, neither the present nor the future, nor any powers, neither height nor depth, nor anything else in all creation, will be able to separate us from the love of God that is in Christ Jesus our Lord."
> —Romans 8:31-35, 38-39

Eternal *insecurity*? No assurance of God's ability to save the one who has come to Christ? God's love for His people can be thwarted, made null and void? Christ can fail to save His people? Not if these words have any meaning at all! *Here* is full reason to lift up praise to God!

Another clear Biblical teaching that is, in effect, denied by those who do not accept the security of the believer, is the role of the Spirit of God in our lives. Listen to what Paul said—

> "And you also were included in Christ when you heard the word of truth, the gospel of your salvation. Having believed, you were marked in him with a seal, the promised Holy Spirit, who is a deposit guaranteeing our inheritance until the redemption of those who are God's possession— to the praise of his glory." —Ephesians 1:13-14

The Holy Spirit is the Father's "pledge money" or guarantee that He is the one who has begun His work, and He will finish His work in this person's life. We are described as God's own possession, and are we to think that God loses His possessions very often? The Holy Spirit is His *mark* of ownership upon us. And what of the power of the Spirit? Cannot the Spirit uphold us and keep us from falling? Does the Spirit fail to apply to us what has been done in our place by Christ? Surely not! Paul told the Corinthians,—

> *"He will keep you strong to the end, so that you will be blameless on the day of our Lord Jesus Christ. God, who has called you into fellowship with his Son Jesus Christ our Lord, is faithful."*   —1 Corinthians 1:8-9

Who keeps the Christian strong? Who has promised that we will stand before Him blameless on the day of the Lord? Who called us into fellowship with Christ? God has done all of this, and Paul believed with all of his heart that God was *faithful*. This does not mean that God has faith in us, but that God is true to His own promises, His own covenants. We can have faith in Him because He is worthy of our trust— He does not change, and will accomplish all that He has promised.

Hidden in Christ

People often ask, "what is your favorite verse in the Bible?" It is, of course, very difficult to identify just *one* passage as my "favorite," but if I had to do so, it would be the third verse of the following—

> *"Since, then, you have been raised with Christ, set your hearts on things above, where Christ is seated on the right hand of God. Set your minds on things above, not on earthly things. For you died, and your life is now hidden with Christ in God."*   —Colossians 3:1-3

Colossians 3:3 teaches a tremendous truth: we have died with

Christ, and our life is now hidden with Christ in God. Our life is no longer simply a matter of earthly existence. Our true life is joined with Christ and is secure in the heavens. Can you see how this is related to the perseverance of the saints? Can you imagine a more *secure* place for one's life than to be hidden with Christ in God? The Greek text indicates that the action of "hiding" is in the perfect tense. This indicates a completed action in the past with abiding results to the present. My life is hidden in Christ and will remain that way. What can possibly touch me there? Will God allow something to enter into my life that would result in my eternal destruction? Why? How? No, I not only have the confidence that I shall remain in Christ for all of eternity, but I also know that whatever touches my life— whether joy or sorrow— has been allowed to do so by my loving Father. This is the confidence of the Christian, a possession and foundation that the world can never take away.

The doctrine of the perseverance of the saints is, quite simply, the doctrine of salvation by grace. If we are saved by God's grace alone, and not by our works, then we must acknowledge the permanence of His work. If we deny eternal security, then we are, in fact, embracing a system of works-salvation. That is the true difference. Paul taught that it is by grace that we have been saved (Ephesians 2:5). The language is rich in this passage, for it emphasizes the continuing truth of our full salvation by grace, both as a completed past action, and a continuing reality in our life. Salvation by grace leads to the perseverance of the saints, for God's sovereign grace cannot possibly fail to do what He desires. Indeed, have we not seen this all along? In each instance, God's grace has been seen to be sufficient and all-powerful. It has been the key to each question we have examined. Grace stands behind everything God has done, and is doing, in this world. But it is a sovereign grace, a powerful grace, a purposeful grace. It is grace that allowed Jude (24-25) to provide the perfect closing for our examination—

> *"To him who is able to keep you from falling and to present you before his glorious presence without fault and with great joy— to the only God and Savior be glory, majesty, power and authority, through Jesus Christ our Lord, before all ages, now and forevermore! Amen."* —Jude v. 24-25

8

A Little History:
Luther, Calvin, Arminius,
and the Council of Dort

*"It is no novelty, then, that I am preaching; no new
doctrine. I love to proclaim those strong old doctrines that
are nicknamed Calvinism, but which are surely and verily
the revealed truth of God as it is in Christ Jesus."*
— *Charles Haddon Spurgeon*

Many Christians today are a people without a history. I grew
up in the middle of the great "fundamentalist" tradition in the
United States, and must admit to having had a rather shallow
view of the history of the Christian Church until my adult years.
For me, and for the majority of others like me, the history of the
Christian Church went back about 50 years or so for all practical purposes. That is not to say that I did not realize that the
Church had been around for nearly two millennia, because I did.
I just didn't have any real idea of what it had been like all those
years, nor did I really have a clear understanding of where I fit
into the whole picture. My father was a minister, and I recall
getting bits and pieces of information about his own father who
was also a minister. But that was as far back as things went. Now,
as one who has had the opportunity and privilege of teaching
Church History, I realize that I had the dreaded disease of
anachronism. What is that? I looked back at history and simply

assumed that things had always been as they were today. I was wrong.

My confusion was even more profound when it came to my Baptist heritage. Some Baptists were very open in claiming that they were *not* Protestants. Why? These folks believed (and many still do) that Baptists had *always* existed, pretty much as Baptists in practice, doctrine, etc. They were very strong in denying that they had ever been part of the Roman Catholic Church, and, since all Protestants left Rome (that is why they were protesting in the first place), then Baptists couldn't be Protestants. I was exposed to literature that attempted to trace a solid line of Baptists all the way back to Pentecost. I did not realize that *most* modern conservative denominations have elements that attempt to do the same thing, and, quite often, end up claiming the same groups[33] as their particular forbearers.

I was not alone in my confusion about my theological and traditional roots. Many others live in the exact same condition of confusion. This explains much of our modern situation, and it says volumes about why so many are willing to so quickly abandon teachings that their ancestors died defending! I knew that I wasn't a Roman Catholic, and I knew that way back when there had been a "Reformation," but I figured that that was only relevant to the Lutherans, since Luther was involved in the whole story somehow. I had no idea how my own tradition was connected with the Reformation, nor where it fit in the entire scheme of things.

Thankfully, some seminaries still require their students to take Church History as a requirement for graduation, and it was in fulfilling this demand that I was directed to the sources of information that answered my many questions about my own theological past. Reading a few good Church History texts, and studying under a tremendously gifted and learned professor of Church History,[34] put things in perspective for me. I soon discovered the deep and abiding debt I owed to such men as Martin Luther, Ulrich Zwingli, Martin Bucer, William Farel, and one John Calvin of Geneva. As this discovery clarified for me many of the issues that surround the doctrines of grace, I am going to briefly share some of the more important aspects of the history of the Reformation that bear upon our discussion.

Martin Luther and Justification by Faith

Martin Luther was a troubled man. He often had fits of depression, and was known for once having thrown his ink-well at the Devil, who was bothering him in a particularly troubling way while he was translating the New Testament into German at the Wartburg Castle.

That may not sound like a very positive description of Luther, but it is in no way meant to be taken in a disparaging way. Luther was troubled long before he refused to bow to the authority of the Roman Catholic Church. He was troubled in a "good" way— he was a man who was troubled about his sin.

If one felt distress about one's sin in the Europe of 1517, the Roman Catholic Church directed you to her own sacraments, penances, and works to find forgiveness. One had to be contrite for one's sins, confess those sins to a priest, and do the works of penance that were assigned by the priest. One could attend Mass, which was believed to be an actual non-bloody sacrifice of Christ, and receive further help in that way, too. But even if one attended a thousand masses and confessed on a regular basis, the dread of long periods of suffering in purgatory hung over every man's head. For quite a while people had been able to buy an "indulgence" letter that removed the penalty for sin and lessened the time spent in purgatory, but pious people received little comfort from such promises.

Luther was one of those pious people. As an Augustinian monk he had done everything that the Church taught regarding finding forgiveness of sins, but these actions did not provide him with peace of mind or conscience. He is said to have spent six hours in the confessional. Now one must realize that there wasn't a whole lot of trouble one could get into in an Augustinian monastery, so anyone who could spend six hours in the confessional was obviously undergoing a good bit of introspection! Millions went about their lives around him, completely satisfied with infrequent confession and a few works of piety, never seeming to feel the same burden of guilt that he did.

In God's providence Luther was sent to teach theology at the new University of Wittenberg. At the same time another Roman Catholic scholar, Desiderius Erasmus, was publishing the very first printed edition of the Greek New Testament. Luther began to examine the meaning of the Roman Catholic concept of "doing penance." The Latin Vulgate translation of the New Testament used this phrase often, but Luther discovered that the original Greek term that the Vulgate had translated "do penance" did not mean that at all. Instead, the Scriptures called us to "repent." The word spoke of a change of the mind, an attitude of the heart, not works of the hands. Slowly the light began to break into the darkness for Martin Luther. He soon came upon that wonderful passage in Paul's epistle to the Romans, "the just shall live by faith" (Romans 1:17).

Justification by faith became Martin Luther's battle-cry. He realized, as the Scriptures taught, that man was totally *unable* to save himself. He further saw that Christ was totally *able* to save man, and that God's grace was the only and sole basis of salvation. While Roman Catholicism paid lip-service to God's grace, in reality grace had been reduced to an aid or help in man's bringing about his own salvation. Luther rejected this concept, and found in the Bible the liberating truth that God actually saves men! Justification by faith, for Luther, was very much the same thing as would be taught with such crystal clarity by the reformer of Geneva twenty years later— John Calvin. What Luther meant by justification by faith is, at its root, the same as Calvin taught with reference to predestination and election. In fact, Luther spoke more often of God's election than

Calvin did! It is simply a strange twist of history that belief in predestination and election has been primarily connected with Calvin (hence the name "Calvinism") rather than Luther. Luther's immediate successor, Melanchthon, drew back from the strong predestinarian theology of Luther, and as a result the entire Lutheran movement was effected thereby. But a quick review of a work that Luther himself felt was one of his most important would convince the unbiased reader that what we have said is true.

The Bondage of the Will (1525) was a response to Desiderius Erasmus, who had written a work defending the freedom of the human will. Luther's response is withering in its criticism of Erasmus' position. The concept of "free-will" is attacked mercilessly by Luther. He clearly asserts (as we have done earlier) that the doctrine of God's omniscience and sovereignty does away with the idea of an autonomous human will:

> The question, therefore, is not difficult; nay, nothing can be more plain to common sense, than that this conclusion is certain, stable, and true:— if it be pre-established from the Scriptures, that God neither errs nor is deceived; then, whatever God foreknows must, of necessity, take place. It would be a difficult question indeed, nay, an impossibility, I confess, if you should attempt to establish, both the prescience of God, and the "Free- will" of man. For what could be more difficult, nay a greater impossibility, than the attempt to prove, that contradictions do not clash; or that a number may, at the same time, be both nine and ten? There is no difficulty on our side of the question, but it is sought for and introduced, just as ambiguity and obscurity are sought for and violently introduced into the Scriptures....Wherefore, the prescience and Omnipotence of God, are diametrically opposite of our "Free-will." And it must be, that either God is deceived in His prescience and errs in His action, (which is impossible) or we act, and are acted upon, according to His prescience and action....This Omnipotence and prescience of God, I say, utterly abolishes the doctrine of "Free-will."[35]

His comments concerning "Free-will" are strong indeed:

> Because, unless you ascribe the whole and all things to "Free-will," as the Pelagians do, the contradictions in the Scriptures are

not altered, merit and reward are taken entirely away, the mercy and justice of God are abolished, and all the difficulties which we try to avoid by allowing the 'certain little ineffective power' to "Free-will," remain just as they were before; as I have already shewn. Therefore, we must come to the plain extreme, deny "Free-will" altogether, and ascribe all unto God! Thus, there will be in the Scriptures no contradictions; and if there be any difficulties, they will be borne with, where they cannot be remedied.[36]

That Luther saw the concept of "Free-will" as part and parcel of the works-salvation system of Rome is plain in this quotation:

But however, that the advocates for "Free-will" deny Christ, is proved, not by this Scripture only, but by their own very way of life. For by their "Free-will," they have made Christ to be unto them no longer a sweet Mediator, but a dreaded Judge, whom they strive to please by the intercessions of the Virgin Mother, and of the Saints; and also, by variously invented works, by rites, ordinances, and vows; by all which, they aim at appeasing Christ, in order that He might give them grace. But they do not believe, that He intercedes before God and obtains grace for them by His blood and grace; as it is here said, "for grace." And as they believe, so it is unto them! For Christ is in truth, an inexorable judge to them, and justly so; for they leave Him, who is a Mediator and most merciful Saviour, and account His blood and grace of less value than the devoted efforts and endeavours of their "Free-will!"[37]

And in concluding his book, Luther wrote,—

For if I believe it to be true, that God fore-knows and fore-ordains all things; that He can be neither deceived nor hindered in His Prescience and Predestination; and that nothing can take place but according to His Will, (which, reason herself is compelled to confess;) then, even according to the testimony of reason herself, there can be no "Free-will"— in man,— in angel,— or in any creature![38]

Why? Why such a strong reaction? Because Luther saw that the concept of "free-will" was in fact an attack upon that precious truth he found in the Bible and that had led to his own personal freedom— justification by faith. Erasmus was doing what Roman Catholicism had done all along. He was placing the final determination of salvation in the hands of man rather than God. Luther denounced this concept, asserting that God is the final determiner, God is the one who saves men. This is the theology that empowered Luther to stand before the Emperor in 1521 and, in so doing, stare-down a power that only a century before had burned John Hus at the stake for believing the same things.

John Calvin and Systematic Theology

In his writings and teachings, Luther was asserting some of the exact same concepts that would be organized and formulated with exacting care by another of the great Reformers, John Calvin. While Luther was the bombastic, fiery preacher, Calvin was the logical, methodical theologian. Luther was the machine-gun, Calvin the sharp-shooter. Luther's thoughts and speech flowed in a raging torrent, and he was not always successful at organizing his views so that they could be clearly presented. Calvin's greatest work, *The Institutes of the Christian Religion*, remains one of the greatest Protestant works of all time, and anyone who has taken the time to read *The Institutes* knows what I am saying when I assert that "the ink is not yet dry," so relevant to our modern times is Calvin's work. *The Institutes* are very carefully organized, and the argument flows on with a force of logic and consistency that has amazed and delighted those who agree with Calvin, and dismayed and disgusted those who do not, for over four centuries.

Calvin's entire theology was based upon the everyday, personal realization of the sovereignty of God in all things. Note this early section from *The Institutes*:

> I call "piety" that reverence joined with love of God which the knowledge of his benefits induces. For until men recognize that they owe everything to God, that they are nourished by his fatherly care, that he is the Author of their every good, that they should seek nothing beyond him— they will never yield him willing service.[39]

Calvin knew that men were likely to reject God's revelation of His own nature in favor of a more "comfortable" perspective:

> Indeed, vanity joined with pride can be detected in the fact that, in seeking God, miserable men do not rise above themselves as they should, but measure him by the yardstick of their own carnal stupidity, and neglect sound investigation; thus out of curiosity they fly off into empty speculations. They do not therefore apprehend God as he offers himself, but imagine him as they have fashioned him in their own presumption.[40]

Just as Luther before him, Calvin emphasized the providence, omnipotence, and omniscience of God in providence:

> And truly God claims, and would have us grant him, omnipotence— not the empty, idle, and almost unconscious sort that the Sophists image, but a watchful, effective, active sort, engaged in ceaseless activity. Not, indeed, an omnipotence that is only a general principle of confused motion, as if he were to command a river to flow through its once-appointed channels, but one that is directed toward individual and particular motions.[41]

And finally, the concept of a doctrine of "free-will" is denied by Calvin as clearly as it was by Luther:

> Therefore, withdrawing from the Kingdom of God, he is at the same time deprived of spiritual gifts, with which he had been furnished for the hope of eternal salvation. From this it follows that he is so banished from the Kingdom of God that all qualities belonging to the blessed life of the soul have been extinguished in him, until he recovers them through the grace of regeneration. Among these are faith, love of God, charity toward neighbor, and zeal for holiness and for righteousness... Similarly the will, because it is inseparable from man's nature, did not perish, but was so bound to wicked desires that it cannot strive after the right.[42]

I have heard John Calvin disparaged and attacked from many a pulpit. I have often thought, upon hearing these attacks, that it is a shame that Calvin's writings are not read more these days. If you are going to attack a man, at least attack him for what he actually said or wrote! Few of those conservative, Bible-believing preachers who so heartily decry the evil of "Calvinism" have ever taken the time to seriously consider what the man had to say. Most assume that all he ever discussed was predestination and election. Nothing could be farther from the truth. The specific discussion of predestination and election does not come until the 21st chapter of Book III of *The Institutes*, and that right on the heels of the longest chapter in the work, the chapter on *prayer!* Calvin's work is *soaked* in Scripture, and draws its overwhelming conviction from the highest view of God's revelation in the Bible. Since Calvin truly desired to be taught by Scripture, his works are marked by the very same *balance* that one finds in the Word. He does not talk about predestination every waking moment. He speaks much of faith, prayer, and doing works that are glorifying to God. Christ is at the center of his teaching, and the Cross is lifted up as the crowning achievement in God's bringing men unto Himself through the gospel.

Jacob Arminius and the Council of Dort

Arminius was born only four years before Calvin's death. He was raised in what might be called the "third generation" of the Reformation. He was highly educated, and even studied in Geneva. He was taught the doctrines of the Reformation, and was fully familiar with the "Calvinistic" formulation of the faith. In 1603, having distinguished himself as a preacher at Amsterdam, he was called to the chair of theology at the university of Leyden. As a result of personal study and reflection, Arminius became convinced that the doctrines of unconditional election and irresistible grace were untenable. He said as much, creating a storm of controversy for denying these doctrines that had, for a short period following the beginning of the Reformation, become predominate in the area of the Netherlands.

Arminius did not attempt to turn the world upside-down with his statements. He was probably surprised by the reaction that came against him. Since he died in 1609, scarcely six years after taking his teaching position at Leyden, Arminius himself did not have a great deal of time to develop his doctrines. He may not even have fully realized how fundamentally his views differed from those of the Reformation. There certainly is little evidence that Arminius wished to undo what had been done in the preceding years!

Arminius' cause, however, was championed by others after his death, leading to inevitable conflict. Some opposed this "Arminian" view for political reasons, and others supported it for the same reasons. The Church and State were still intimately connected, and theological debate did not take place without a good dosage of political influence as well. The Arminian party presented to the Dutch parliament an outline of their views, called the "Remonstrance", and they were quickly dubbed the "Remonstrants." We will not argue here whether the Remonstrants went beyond what Arminius himself taught. As a result of the teachings of the Remonstrants, a national synod was held in the city of Dort from November of 1618 till May of 1619. During the 154 sessions of this council, the arguments of the Remonstrants were examined, and rejected. In their place what came to be known as the "five points of Calvinism" was presented.

The story of Arminius and his rejection of God's sovereign grace and election should teach us a number of things. First, Arminius was one of the first generation of "Protestants" proper. He was raised within the thought structure of the Reformation, even in its infancy. Yet, he rejected doctrines that, as we have seen, are simply foundational to the entire Reformed concept of the gospel. What does this mean? It means that while we have every responsibility to teach our children the truth of God's Word, we can *never* assume that simply being exposed to the truth will result in an acceptance of that truth. God's grace must reveal these truths to the heart— no amount of education can accomplish what the Spirit Himself must do.

The most important lesson to learn from Arminius is a negative one. No matter how we might attempt to understand someone's desire to "safeguard" in their mind the "justice" of God, we must never place our thoughts above the revealed Word of God. We have seen that the Bible teaches the doctrines that Arminius rejected, and that without in the least bit compromising the justice of God. We cannot place our own desires above the Word of God. By doing so, Arminius, in reality, undid everything that the Reformation worked to accomplish. His teachings struck at the *heart* of the gospel of Christ, and placed those innumerable souls who follow his teachings today right back upon the exact same ground upon which the theology of Rome had been built long before.

The Theology of the Reformation

Certainly Calvin and Luther were not the only people who contributed to the theology of the Reformation. But in this short chapter we are not trying to present an exhaustive history of that tumultuous time. Instead, we provide the above information simply for the purpose of demonstrating the truth of the following assertion: *It was not Arminian theology that provided the strength and power of the Reformation; it was "Reformed" or "Calvinistic" theology that called men to stand up for the truth of the gospel against the tyranny of Rome.* Modern evangelicals need to recognize that Arminianism is, at its very core, a *return* to the very principles that the Reformation fought against in the first place! While the outward manifestations might differ, Arminianism and Roman Catholicism stand hand-in-hand in opposing God's sovereign grace in salvation! Both place the final decision of the outcome of an individual's life completely in the hands of the man himself, and in so doing, deny God His rightful role as Creator and Sovereign of the universe. Most of modern evangelicalism does not, in reality, have anything to say to Rome, simply because it has compromised on the central issue of God's grace!

Further, since Arminianism is, when taken to its logical conclusions, antithetical to simple Christian theism,[43] those who
embrace this system find themselves incapable of *consistently*
dealing with the philosophies of man, simply because they have
embraced some of the most fundamental concepts of those philosophies rather than accepting the revelation of the sovereign
God! In a vain effort to "win" men by seeking to avoid offense,
the strong doctrines of God as Creator and Sustainer of the universe are left to the side, and the battle is joined on the
homeground of the atheist or secular humanist. The gospel is
compromised in the interest of defending it! Such simply ought
not to be.

Many today are calling for a second Reformation, and surely
we can understand the need for it. But such a Reformation will
require some very tough stands by those seeking the truth.
Worldly acceptance and friendship cannot have any place of
importance for those who wish to be used of God in such a
movement. Those who call themselves "Protestants" but who
deny the foundational Biblical teachings about God *will have to
be identified for what they really are*— not to be mean, but so
that the truth can be clearly distinguished from error. Furthermore, the Christian Church will need to reject the metho-
dologies of men and trust solely in the Spirit of God to bring
the "results." We must seek God's honor and glory, rather than
numbers or worldly measures of "success."

9

Conclusion

"We shall never be clearly persuaded, as we ought to be, that our salvation flows from the wellspring of God's free mercy until we come to know his eternal election, which illumines God's grace by this contrast: that he does not indiscriminately adopt all into the hope of salvation but gives to some what he denies to others." — *John Calvin*

I will not argue that what has come before differs a great deal from much of popular belief today. That, sadly, is a given. However, I desire to warn the reader that truth is not determined by majority vote. In fact, truth is rarely popular, and is hardly ever in the majority. Truth is determined by God, and we know His truth through His Word.

The issues of "Calvinism" are normally identified as "options" by those who wish to avoid having to make the difficult decisions that are forced upon someone by the Word of God. "Those are side-issues," we are told, "and should not take up our thinking." If someone begins to seek consistency in their faith, and to seek answers to the difficult issues we have looked at in this book, they are often counseled to not get "too deep" into these things. "Just tell folks about Jesus" is what we hear.

Yet, the Holy Spirit of God, the Spirit of wisdom, inspired the writers of Scripture to not just make brief mention of such things as God's sovereign nature, His election of a people in Christ, and man's deadness in sin, but to speak much of those things! We have seen that a recognition of the true nature of grace as sovereign grace is foundational to a proper understanding of the entire gospel itself!

We are surrounded on all sides by false teachings that exalt man and abase God. Works-salvation systems, which mock the grace of God and the saviorhood of Jesus Christ, are to be heard on radio stations and seen on television channels every hour of the day. Why? Why does the Church so easily accept such teachings, or at the very least, attempt to ignore them? And why has the Church bought into Madison Avenue techniques of evangelism, resulting in the down-playing of the "offensive" elements of the gospel of Christ? Quite simply, the truth of the gospel has been traded for that which gives "success" by human standards. It does not promote "church growth" to point out error amongst those who believe in works-salvation. People will not watch your television program if you are constantly reminding them of their need for God's grace. People want to be made to feel good about themselves. They want their egos stroked. The gospel of Christ doesn't do that.

The Church of Jesus Christ must continually be reformed by the Spirit of God applying the truth of God found in the Word of God. This is a never-ending process, thanks be to God. The doctrines of grace are, quite simply, the doctrines of the gospel of Christ. They are not "side issues" whose teaching can be ignored. The Church's power resides in the gospel, for the gospel is the power of God unto salvation. The Church must *always* seek after the purity of the Gospel of Christ. The world will continually put pressure upon the Church to compromise the gospel, to "tone it down" in this way or that. But God's Word does not change, and God's word will always call His Church back to the gospel.

The culture in which we live is not challenged by a proclamation that compromises on the central issues. A God who cannot save outside of human effort, who has actually put Himself in a situation where His entire effort to save man might just fail if man does not help Him out, does not call men to reverence and worship. Men inherently know that the true and living God is far greater than the caricature of Him that is presented so often today. If we desire to see God glorified, and if we desire to see our world changed, we must abandon human standards of what is right and wrong, and go back to the revelation that is found in God's Word. We must speak the truth boldly, and in love. But to speak the truth we must know the truth, and confess the truth.

The vast majority of those that I know personally who do not embrace the doctrines of God's sovereign grace do not do so out of malice. In fact, most only know a little bit about what they reject. Theirs is a rejection based upon ignorance, not knowledge. For those fellow believers, I hope this book has been a help. I believe I am consistent with my faith in saying that I cannot argue you into accepting the doctrines of God's grace. I believe that God must open a person's eyes, and instill in a person's heart a love for His sovereignty and holiness. I pray He will do that for you. But I am not God, nor can I instill in you something that comes from the Holy Spirit alone. If God is calling you to really consider these things, and to search the Scriptures (Acts 17:11), then be obedient to Him, and ask Him to reveal Himself to you. As one who has taught these doctrines to many, I realize that these issues can be "painful" ones. Often I am told that the doctrine of predestination "frightens" people, and that they are hesitant to accept the concept of God's absolute sovereignty. There is normally a process that one goes through, struggling with each doctrine, thinking it through, searching the Scriptures, and praying. This is proper and good. I recall one woman saying to me months after first hearing these doctrines that her entire outlook— how she viewed God, her fellow man, even herself— had been radically altered and changed. "Looking at the world in a God-centered way rather than a man-centered way has taken time, but the results have been incredible."

Others, sadly, oppose the doctrines of grace out of less than pure motives. No formulation of the Christian faith more vehemently denies and destroys the concept of human merit or works-salvation than the Reformed. Those who present a human-centered concept of salvation, then, hate Calvinism simply because it is the consistent presentation of God's grace and man's need. It cuts the very foundation out from under their system. Calvin wrote,

> "If— to make it clear that our salvation comes about solely from God's mere generosity— we must be called back to the course of election, those who wish to get rid of all this are obscuring as maliciously as they can what ought to have been gloriously and vociferously proclaimed, and they tear humility up by the very roots.[44]

I have often experienced great frustration when I have seen people attempting to share the gospel with those involved in false religious systems. They truly desire to see the lost saved, but their unfamiliarity with, or their rejection of, the doctrines of grace leads them to compromise on the very issues that are the most important! They end up agreeing about man's abilities and God's limitations! And they wonder why those to whom they speak cannot see the differences?

We are to seek to bring God glory in all things. My friend, God is not glorified by preaching and teaching and evangelism that ignores major elements of what *He* considered worthy of revealing to us! The gospel is not ours to edit, it is ours to proclaim. Men will be offended. We know that. We dare not attempt to avoid discomfort when the purity of the gospel is at stake. The Bible teaches that God has elected to bring certain men unto Himself. We have seen this clearly presented in the pages of Holy Scripture. Will we live in harmony with this truth? Will we accept God's grace toward us, and thank Him for His mercy? It is my prayer that each and every one who takes the time to consider these things will bow before the Father in earnest thankfulness and join the heavenly chorus of worship—

> "Then I heard every creature in heaven and on earth and
> under the earth and on the sea, and all that is in them,
> singing:
>
>> 'To him who sits on the throne
>> and to the Lamb be praise and honor and glory and
>> power, for ever and ever!' "
>>
>> —Revelation 5:13

10

"Foreknowledge"— Its New Testament Usage

"For whom He did foreknow, He also predestined to be conformed to the image of His Son, so that He might be the firstborn of many brothers. And whom He did predestine, these He also called; and whom He called, these He also justified; and whom He justified, these He also glorified."   —Romans 8:29-30

This incredible passage, known as the "Golden Chain of Redemption," has long held great fascination for men and women of God. Yet, the truth it proclaims has, for the most part, been obscured all-too-often by a misunderstanding of one of the very first terms encountered, that being "foreknew." What does this term mean? Roman Catholic theologians, lacking the concept of salvation by grace through faith, and the attendant concept of the sovereignty of God in salvation (election), view the term as referring to God's "foresight" of future events; that is, God, knowing the future, "chooses" those whom He knows will be pliable to His will and who will repent from their sins and turn to Him. This is the same position held by Arminians as well. For example, Dr. Curtis Hutson, editor of *The Sword of the Lord*, has written a small booklet entitled "Why I Disagree with All Five

Points of Calvinism." Dr. Hutson' s comments on this point are very representative of the Arminian perspective: "God in His foreknowledge knows who will trust Jesus Christ as Savior, and He has predestined to see that they are justified and glorified." In other words, God elects on the basis of the actions of man (though seen in the future) rather than on the sole basis of His own will and purpose. This, we are told, is what "foreknowledge" means— a simple knowing of future events, with the result that certain actions can be taken on the basis of those future events.

But, we must ask, is this what the Bible teaches? Are we taught in Scripture that God responds to the actions of men, even when those actions are future? Or does the term "foreknowledge" mean this at all?

To answer these questions, we must first understand the process of determining what a word in the New Testament actually meant to the writer and his audience. Frequently modern writers assume that the English translation carries all of the range and depth of meaning of the original Greek or Hebrew term when in fact it does not. Also, there is great danger in "pushing" the meaning of the English term back onto the Greek or Hebrew word. What matters is not what an English word means today, but what a Greek or Hebrew word meant back then!

So, to find out what the Bible means when it speaks of God's "foreknowledge," we must look at the usage of the Greek term itself; we must see how it functions in the New Testament, and, just as importantly, we must discover whether it has been influenced by the Old Testament as well.

The Greek term translated by the noun "foreknowledge" is προγνωσις (prognosis). The verbal form, προγινωσκω (proginosko) is the term found in Romans 8:29 above, as well as in Romans 11:2, and 1 Peter 1:20 (this study will focus only on the usage of these terms in regards to God). The noun form is found in Acts 2:23 and 1 Peter 1:2. On first glance the meaning, as the Greek term is a compound of προ (before) and γινωσκω (to know), seems fairly simple: to know beforehand. But before such a simple answer is accepted, let's look at what it means "to know."

Anyone familiar with the range of meaning and usage of the terms γινωσκω and οιδα (another term meaning "to know") in Paul's writings knows that the nuances of meaning found in these terms is anyt in but easily defined. Therefore, the better part of wisdom is to ask, "is the term 'to know' in the Old Testament relevant to the meaning of the same term in the New?" To find out, let's look at the OT term "to know."

The basic Hebrew term translated "to know" in the Old Testament is *yada*. Both Greek terms noted above (γινωσκω / οιδα) are used to translate this one Hebrew word; γινωσκω is used over 500 times as the translation of *yada* in the Septuagint (LXX). And what does this term mean in Hebrew? Does it refer simply to having intellectual knowledge? No indeed! When the Hebrew speaks of God's knowledge, something far more than just bare cognizance of facts is in view. Let's look at some passages where this will be seen and see if some of the fuller meaning of yada can be discovered.

"Before I formed you in the womb I knew (*yada*) you, before you were born I consecrated you; I have appointed you a prophet to the nations" (Jeremiah 1:5). Here God says that He 'knew" Jeremiah even before He formed the prophet in the womb. Does this mean that God simply had knowledge of the future actions of Jeremiah? Clearly not, for the parallelism of the passage indicates that the knowing is to be understood as being synonymous with God's consecration of him and His appointing him as a prophet to the nations. Hence, the term refers to an action on God's part in choosing in regards to Jeremiah. God is active in this knowing, this choosing. The object of His knowing is not a fact, but a person. God's *yada* of Jeremiah is personal. Is this kind of understanding a common feature of Hebrew thinking? Indeed it is! For the Hebrew writers, knowledge is very personal.

One cannot know something truly in the Hebrew system of thought simply by standing afar off and thinking about an object. Knowledge is personal. When Adam knew Eve in Genesis 4:1, the result was the conception of a child. Obviously, then, this "knowing" of Eve by Adam was far more than a simple understanding of her existence—his *yada* of his wife was intensely personal. But when we speak of God's knowing someone, we are speaking of His entering into personal relationship with that individual.

This is seen very clearly in Yahweh's encounter with Moses in Exodus 33. In verse 17 we read God's saying to Moses, "I will also do this thing of which you have spoken; for you have found favor in My sight, and I have known (*yada*) you by name." Earlier Moses had indicated that God had spoken these words to him before (v. 12). Surely we here see that God is not simply saying "I know your name" but that something far more personal is in view here. The knowing of Moses' name is very personal; God is indicating His gracious decision to enter into a very special and personal relationship with Moses. The fact that this passage figures so prominently in Paul's discussion of election in Romans 9:15 is surely significant as well, for if Paul connects verse 19 of this chapter with God's predestination in Romans 9, surely his usage of "foreknow" in Romans 8 is drawn from here, too.

The continued emphasis upon the personal nature of the object of God's knowledge is seen as well in Amos 3:2, where the nation of Israel, as God's special covenant people, is addressed: "You only have I known (*yada*) among all the nations of the earth." Here God asserts that He has known only the people of Israel. Again, bare factual knowledge cannot possibly be the meaning, as God surely knows that other peoples exist, for He created them! Instead, the word "know" means 'to choose." Both the *New American Standard Bible* and the *New International Version* render *yada* here as "chosen." So prevalent is this sense of the Hebrew term when in reference to God that the *Theological Dictionary of the Old Testament* (5:468) comments, "We find yd' (*yada*) in Amos 3:2 as an expression for the special relationship between Yahweh and Israel or election to service... In Exodus 33:12,17 yd' characterize(s) the special election (and call)... In Jeremiah 1:5 the appointment of Jeremiah to prophetic office is characterized by yd'... (since) long before his birth Jeremiah had been chosen as a prophet."

Does the emphasis upon the active choice of God to enter into a personal relationship with an individual as an emphasis of the concept of "knowing m the Old Testament come through in the New? It most certainly does! For example, when the Lord Jesus refers to His sheep, He asserts, "I am the good shepherd; and I know My own, and My own know Me, even as the Father knows Me and I know the Father; and I lay down My life for the sheep" (John 10:14-15). Again, simple knowledge of data is surely not what is in mind. Here "knowing" refers to personal relationship. The same is to be found elsewhere in Matthew 7:23, when the Lord Jesus dismisses the ungodly from before the judgment seat with the words, "And then I will declare to them, 'I never knew you; depart from Me, you who work lawlessness.'" Again, Jesus certainly had an intellectual knowledge of these people, but they did not have a personal relationship with Him. And the "firm foundation of God stands, having this seal, 'the Lord knows those who are His'" (2 Timothy 2:19).

Hence, we have seen that "to know" in Scripture, especially when it is God who is doing the "knowing" and when the object of this "knowing" is personal (a person, or a people, as in Israel), refers not to a knowledge of data and facts, but a personal relationship between God and the "knowee." With this concept in mind, let us now look at the concept of God's foreknowledge in the New Testament.

Above we cited Romans 8:29-30. As we look at this passage we note that again the object of God's action of foreknowing is a person (or a people if we take the plurality of all men and women who are to be saved). We do not here see God knowing actions but rather people. God is not the passive recipient of knowledge of future events, but the active one who is foreknowing. This is God's choice, God's action in entering into a personal relationship with His creation. In this context, προγινωσκω refers to God's gracious choice to enter into the special relationship of Redeemer to those who are the object of His love, the elect (v. 33).

This understanding of *proginosko* is confirmed by its usage in Romans 11:2. "God has not rejected His people whom He foreknew." This is spoken about the people of Israel. Surely no truth is more clearly proclaimed in the Old Testament than that found in Deuteronomy 7:6-7: "For you are a holy people to Yahweh your God; Yahweh your God has chosen you to be a people for His own possession out of all the peoples who are on the face of the earth. Yahweh did not set His love on you or choose you because you were more in number than any of the peoples, for you were the fewest of all peoples...." God chose Israel freely and without any reference to their actions, merits, or anything else. But, if the common meaning of foreknowledge as seen in most modern understandings is used here, we would be forced into the absurd statement that God chose Israel because He foresaw that Israel would choose Him! Can anyone with even the slightest familiarity with the history of the nation of Israel make such a statement? Surely not! God's election of the people of Israel was based upon His gracious decision to enter into covenant relationship with them, not on the basis of His foreseeing their actions or attitudes.

The personal nature of foreknowledge is seen as well in 1 Peter 1:20, where Christ is said to have been "foreknown" before the foundation of the earth. Here again, election, choosing, personal relationship—all these elements that we have traced through the Old Testament are found to appear in the New.

The noun *prognosis* is found in two places in the New Testament. 1 Peter 1:2 is the first of these: "(who are)... chosen according to the foreknowledge of God the Father, by the sanctifying work of the Spirit, unto the obedience and sprinkling of the blood of Jesus Christ; grace and peace be multiplied to you." Just as it is revealed in Romans 8:29, the Biblical order is foreknown, then elected (predestined). But, as we have seen, this is a sovereign decision by God wherein He enters a personal relationship with the object of His foreknowledge. Before we even existed, God graciously entered into relationship with us. What incredible mercy!

The second passage in which God's foreknowledge is found (using the noun form *prognosis*) is Acts 2:23: "this One, delivered up by the predetermined plan and foreknowledge of God, you nailed to a cross by the hands of godless men and put Him to death." At first glance it might seem as if this usage contradicts what has been seen before; that is, it looks as if here the *action* of the delivering up of Christ is what is foreknown, not Christ Himself, in opposition to what has been said,— that God's foreknowledge is always in regards to people, not things or actions. But a closer look at the passage reveals that the object of God's foreknowledge is indeed Christ. Hence it was according to God's will and choice that Christ was delivered up. Surely we are not going to say that God simply looked into the future and saw what Christ would do; God is the very origin and source of Christ's work; it was His will and plan. He is not reacting to some future event in sending Christ; God is the one who decided to send Christ.

So what have we seen? We have discovered that the Biblical presentation of God's knowledge is consistent between the Old and New Testaments; that in the OT God's "knowledge" (*yada*) involves His gracious choice and selection of a person or people; that this continues on in the NT when we find that God's foreknowledge (*prognosis*) refers to God's gracious, merciful and solely sovereign choice to enter into personal relationship with a person. In the case of Christ, this is referred to His work in providing salvation; He is "known" as the Redeemer. In reference to the elect, this is referred to God's action in bringing them into relationship with Him. As Kittel's *Theological Dictionary of the New Testament* says, "In the NT 'proginoskein' is referred to God. His foreknowledge, however, is an election or foreordination of His people... or Christ" (I:715). The mere concept of simply having knowledge of future events has been seen to be inconsistent with the NT usage, and so must be rejected.

What then can we conclude? That God's election of individuals to salvation is free and sovereign; His action is *not* based upon anything in the creature—either of merit or action. God's action in predestination is based solely on Himself and His own will. This is vitally important in many ways; our theology of God will be seriously compromised if we accept the concept of God's being dependent upon the actions of creatures in the creation of His decrees. Not only this, but a gospel that bases salvation upon the choice and action of man dishonors God and debilitates the Church. Let us stand firm in the proclamation of the Apostle Paul, "It is from Him that you are in Christ Jesus, who became to us wisdom from God, and righteousness and sanctification and redemption, so that just as it has been written, 'Let him who boasts, boast in the Lord'" (1 Corinthians 1:30-31).

11

Denial of the Doctrines of Grace Leads to Grave Error

Here we will present quotations from two popular writers who have chosen to oppose the doctrines of grace as found in Reformed theology, and will see that the rejection of these truths, based as they are upon divine revelation, leads to further denials of basic Christian doctrine. We will then provide a study of the theology of God as presented in Isaiah chapters 40 through 45, a "treasure trove" of truth on the magnificent God who has deemed it proper to reveal Himself to us.

First, we must recognize that there are different "levels" of Arminianism. Many, many people would deny being a "Calvinist" and would end up in the Arminian camp for no other reason than there isn't anywhere else for them to go. Many "Arminians" I have talked to were not familiar with the issues and had certainly not taken the time to think through the ramifications of their beliefs. So, when we assert, as we will below, that consistent Arminianism leads to a denial of Christian theism, we are not saying that every Arminian does not believe in such things as the sovereignty of God or the existence of His providence. What we are saying is that if they were to take the time to follow their rejection of the Reformed doctrines to their conclusion, they would end up, as many have, denying such concepts as God's eternality, creatorship, omnipotence, and omniscience.

We have asserted, in the body of this book, that belief in God's absolute sovereignty, and the resultant belief in the doctrines of grace, is *forced* upon us by 1) a dedication to the absolute authority of the Bible as the Word of God, and 2) a consistent, whole reading of the Scriptures. The Bible teaches us certain things about the existence and attributes of God, and these things are foundational to our understanding of all else. We are theocentric, meaning that our view of God takes center place to all else. It is highly dangerous to define reality in terms of humanity rather than God Himself. It is the common experience of man to attempt to define God in terms of himself, rather than defining himself in terms of God. We feel that the Reformed view does not do this, while the Arminian concept does.

Arminian Statements

Clark Pinnock wrote an introductory essay for the book, *The Grace of God, the Will of Man*,[45] entitled *From Augustine to Arminius: A Pilgrimage in Theology*. Pinnock has moved from a Reformed perspective to an Arminian one. It should be noted that he has gone a good bit beyond the average "Arminian in the pew", for Pinnock has taken in concepts from another system of theology, known as *process theology*. We shall discuss this philosophical view below. Early on in the essay Pinnock discusses the first "hole" which developed in his former (Calvinistic) view. He declared that the concept of *eternal security* was unbiblical, and from that point the entire fabric of the system began to unravel for him. Under a section entitled *Widening Implications*, he asserts that the "horrible decree" spoken of by Calvin, specifically, the decree of reprobation, did not exist at all. With reference to this, he wrote:

"Calvin's logic was impeccable as usual; God wills whatever happens, so if there are to be lost people, God must have willed it. It was as logically necessary as it was morally intolerable.[46]

The purpose here is not to refute Pinnock's comments on reprobation. Instead, I wish to point out an underlying theme that can be seen throughout the citations from Arminian and process theologians. Pinnock identifies God's decree of reprobation as "morally intolerable." But what exactly is morally intolerable? To answer such a question we must know what is moral, and what is not; but aren't we dependent upon the revelation of God in His Word for this knowledge? Can we depend upon our own consciences which are warped and distorted by sin to determine what is moral, or for that matter morally *intolerable*? Certainly not! Who are we to judge God's actions? The issue quite simply is this: is reprobation consistent with the Bible's teaching? Pinnock's and similiar views are nothing more than incipient humanism determining theology, albeit very poor theological beliefs. If God has created all things, including time itself, then such concepts as predestination, election, providence, and reprobation are impossible to avoid. Therefore contemporary Arminian writers like Pinnock must jettison these concepts, realizing that to accept them (as many Arminians do) is to become inconsistent and illogical. Pinnock wrote,

"Having created human beings with relative autonomy alongside himself, God voluntarily limits his power to enable them to exist and to share in the divine creativity. God invites humans to share in deciding what the future will be."[47]

The future is an unknown quantity, something that is not determined solely by the will of God, but by what might be called a "partnership" between the Creator and the created. We have no idea what a "relative autonomy" is, since the two terms, placed together, create an oxymoron. But we note that for such a "relatively autonomous" being such as man to exist requires a limitation of the power of God. This *limitation* then results in man becoming somewhat of a "co-creator" with God, or, as

Pinnock put it, his sharing "in the divine creativity."

One does not have to work hard at seeing how such orthodox concepts as God's immutability, eternality, omniscience and omnipotence are seriously compromised by such concepts. We have to assert, however, that a full and consistent Arminianism must result in beliefs such as these.

What other orthodox concepts are threatened by the Arminian rejection of the sovereignty of God? Pinnock takes up the atonement of Christ a little later in his essay:

> Obviously it required me to reduce the precision in which I understood the substitution to take place. Christ's death on behalf of the race evidently did not automatically secure for anyone an actual reconciled relationship with God, but made it possible for people to enter into such a relationship by faith.[48]

Shortly thereafter Pinnock encourages us to "view the atonement as an act of judicial demonstration rather than a strict or quantitative substitution as such."[49] While Pinnock claims that a universal atonement is the Biblical view, we note that his comments are directly contradictory to Hebrews 9:12, which states that Christ *did* obtain eternal redemption by His death, and Colossians 1:20, where Christ did accomplish reconciliation through His cross. Pinnock must jettison the substitutionary nature of the death of Christ to maintain his human autonomy. The gospel itself becomes something that is defined by man.

As Pinnock continues his story, he moves on to assert what he calls "Free-Will Theism." What must we believe if we make our own supposed free-will most important? What kind of theism do we end up embracing? Here are some quotations:

> Immutable in his self-existence, the God of the Bible is relational and changeable in his interaction with his creatures. The Word "became" flesh— praise God for his changing unchangeability![50]

> What I came to realize at this stage was how strongly the Bible itself speaks of God as operating from within time and history.[51]

> Decisions not yet made do not exist anywhere to be known even by God. They are potential— yet to be realized but not yet actual.

God can predict a great deal of what we will choose to do, but not all of it, because some of it remains hidden in the mystery of human freedom.[52]

The gravity of these statements cannot be over-emphasized. Pinnock can speak of God as "immutable" yet mutable, using such phrases as "his changing unchangeability." What do such things mean? This kind of language is purposefully confusing and vague. It results in an inability to communicate truth about God. How can such a concept about God be communicated to men? Do we ever find the Psalmist praising God for His "changeableness?" Is such a God fit to be the sure foundation of the Christian Church? Is this a Biblical teaching? Hardly. Then we read what is quite clearly a denial of divine omniscience, based upon the concept that the "mystery of human freedom" means that human decisions are simple potentialities that cannot be known by anyone— including God!

Pinnock's writing is consistent with the denial of the foundations of the doctrines of grace. Both God's absolute sovereignty and eternality, as well as the creatureliness of man himself, is seriously compromised by this kind of teaching. But we do not believe that the resultant system has any right to call itself "Biblical" by any means. In fact, we are reminded of the story related by R.C. Sproul in his fine work, *Chosen by God*.[53] While teaching on the Westminster Confession of Faith's first article, "God, from all eternity, did, by the most wise and holy counsel of His own will, freely, and unchangeably ordain whatsoever comes to pass," Sproul asked how many in the room disagreed with the statement. A number of hands went up. He then asked how many convinced atheists were in attendance. No hands went up. Sproul asserted, "Everyone who raised his hand to the first question should also have raised his hand to the second question." Sproul is asserting that sovereignty is a necessary aspect of simple theism. God, to be God, must be sovereign. So, the statements being made by Pinnock and others are not simply aimed against Calvinism as such. We assert that they are aimed against any logical or meaningful kind of *true theism*!

Another popular work on the subject is *God's Foreknowledge and Man's Free Will* by Richard Rice.[54] Rice presents what he calls an "open view of God." What does this entail? We have already seen much of what he has to say in Pinnock's materials, but Rice is very candid in admitting that his view is similar to "process theology," the doctrine of God put forth by such men as Alfred North Whitehead and Charles Hartshorne. He adds that there are also differences, which is true. But we feel that the differences are minor compared to the similarities. Rice writes:

> "The concept of God proposed here shares the process view that God's relation to the temporal world consists in a succession of concrete experiences, rather than a single timeless perception."[55]

In other words, God is not transcendent over time, existing *outside* of time, but is experiencing time as we experience time. The future is future to Him, the past is past, and in the present He is learning, growing, experiencing. He continues on,—

> "It conceives God as both absolute and relative, necessary and contingent, eternal and temporal, changeless and changing. It attributes one element in each pair of contrasts to the appropriate aspect of God's being— the essential divine character or the concrete divine experience."

It seems that this view tells us that God, in His being, is one thing, and in His "experience" is quite another— in fact, the opposite. In His being, He is unchangeable, yet in His experience, changeable. It is easy to understand how the orthodox theologian can simply say, "This is double-talk!" Couplets of opposites joined together may give the *appearance* of some "deep wisdom" on the part of the writer, but, in reality, they result in nothing but meaningless gibberish.

The fact that Rice is following the God of human experience as his final authority (rather than the Word of God) is clearly presented in the following quotation:

> An open view of reality requires an open conception of God's relation to the world. For if God's knowledge perfectly reflects reality, and if reality is dynamic, open, and constantly developing, then the same must be true of God's knowledge. It, too, is dynamic, open, and constantly developing. The contents of God's experience, therefore, are not fixed or static. They are constantly increased as new data pass from the developing world into the mind of God.[56]

Note well what is said. Humans perceive the world as "open" for it is "dynamic" and "constantly developing." Since we supposedly experience reality in this way, then, Rice asserts, God must be related to the world in the way that *we* perceive it! What tremendous audacity to limit God on the basis of man's perceptions! Rice then directly teaches that God *"is learning"* as "new data pass from the developing world into the mind of God." No perfect knowledge, no omniscience, and why? How can Rice teach this? Does the Bible support this conclusion? Certainly not! Man's experience, the god of all human wisdom, is his only authority. Robert Morey was not wrong to assert that Rice "must be judged as being as heretical as the Jehovah's Witnesses, who also deny that God knows all the details of the future."[57]

One of the most precious possessions of the Church down through the ages has been the promises of God. We have always trusted that what God has promised, He can perform. But such promises are little comfort if God does not have both the power and the knowledge to bring them to pass. A limited God, as Rice and Pinnock present, cannot give true promises. This can be seen in Rice's frightening discussion of God's taking "risks." He writes,—

> "The open view of God allows us to attribute risk to the divine experience, thus enriching our appreciation of His love for us. There are at least two significant points in which we can think of God as assuming a risk. One is Creation. The other in the Incarnation.
>
> In creating morally free beings, God left the future of the world partially indefinite. Their free choices would complete the future."[58]

God took a "risk" in creation, because, it seems, the end result may not be the best! We shall see that this is *exactly* what "process theology" teaches below. Rice then said:

> Again at the Incarnation God undertook the risk that His Son would fail in His struggle with temptation....In giving His Son for man's salvation, God was not merely expressing His disposition toward humanity. He was also running the risk of permanently disastrous consequences to the Godhead itself.[59]

Anyone who has read the Bible to any depth must recoil at the concept that God, in sending the Son, was "risking" abject failure on the part of Christ, and, in fact, was risking the disruption, even the destruction, of the Godhead itself! Is this Jehovah God? No one can possibly believe so.

The Heresy of Process Theology

We have already noted the similarities between the statements made by Arminian writers and "process theology." Process theologians see God as a growing, changing being, one who is in "process." God experiences time in concrete, distinct "packets" of time. He does not have "coercive" power over creation, but merely has "persuasive" power in attempting to convince the creation (which, it is alleged, has the ability to decide whether to accept God's "persuasion" or not; and this ability to "decide" is even extended to inanimate matter!) to be the best it can be. That which is good in each packet of time is absorbed into the divine being. That which is not good is sloughed off. Obviously, the deity of process theology bears no resemblance whatsoever to the Christian God revealed in Scripture.

Charles Hartshorne's writings have given form to modern expressions of process theology. In his book, *The Divine Relativity*,[60] Hartshorne shows how completely humanism, with its chief doctrine of the centrality of man and his experience, is at the source of process theology. Using many of the same arguments that Paul refuted in Romans 9, Hartshorne ridicules the orthodox concept of God, and says,—

"Would they not do better to take a fresh start (as indeed many have done) and admit that we have no good religious reason for positing the notion of providence as an absolute contriving of all events according to a completely detailed plan embracing all time?...The properly constituted man does not want to "rely" upon God to arrange all things, including our decisions, in accordance with a plan of all events which fixes every least detail with reference to every other that ever has happened or ever "is to" happen. How many atheists must have been needlessly produced by insistence upon this arbitrary notion, which after all is invariably softened by qualifications surreptitiously introduced *ad hoc* when certain problems are stressed!" [61]

One hardly needs to note that there is no concept of Scriptural authority in Hartshorne! The "properly constituted" man, rather than waiting upon the Lord and contemplating His law, does not want to "rely" upon the omnipotent and Sovereign God! Surely this tells us something about what Hartshorne thinks the "properly constituted man" is! He is a humanist's humanist, a practical atheist to the core. Then he goes on to allege that the proclamation of the sovereign providence of God is responsible for the production of atheists! Seemingly, we will have less atheists if we quit teaching what the Bible says!

Lewis S. Ford[62] is another process theologian whose words should help us to understand the danger of rejecting the Biblical revelation of God for a production of our limited human wisdom (if such a term can be used in this context). Following Whitehead, the father of all process theologians, Ford writes,

"The concept of divine coercive power, both in its pure and modified forms, has led to grave difficulties." [63]

"Coercive power," for the process theologian, is power over the creation itself, to be contrasted with mere "persuasive power." Ford continues,—

"Consider the extreme instance in which God is conceived as exerting unlimited coercive power, thereby controlling and determining all things. God is the master potter, moulding the clay of the world by the force of his creative activity, except that God has no need of any clay with which to work; he makes his own." [64]

This is the "extreme" instance, according to Ford. Yet, what is described is nothing but the Biblical presentation of God! God does indeed have unlimited coercive power (Psalm 115:3, 135:6, Isaiah 43:13) and He *does* control and determine all things! He is the master potter (Romans 9:21-24). The utterly anti-Biblical, and, anyone would have to therefore admit, anti-Christian teaching of process theology should be plain for all to see. But it gets worse! Here is a classic passage where man forms God in man's own image:

> "Most views of divine power are less extreme, but they all share the same basic defects insofar as they ascribe coercive power to God. To the extent that God exercises such power, creaturely freedom is restricted, the reality of the world is diminished, and the divine experience is impoverished. Creaturely freedom is all important, for without it God is deprived of the one thing the world can provide which God cannot alone have: a genuine social existence." [65]

So according to Ford: divine experience, creaturely freedom and the very reality of the world are dependent upon God's *not* exercising a coercive power. This "creaturely freedom is all important," according to Ford, for without such freedom, he asserts, God could not have a "genuine social existence." The Christian should reject all of this as nothing more than another human attempt to create a god in his own image (which is idolatry, by definition). Ford later states, contradictorily, that even if God needed this "genuine social existence", (which supposedly only an *un*-coerced mankind can give Him), He has always had a social existence in the Trinity from all eternity. A few more double-speak quotes from Ford should allow us to move on:

> "The image of God as the craftsman, the cosmic watchmaker, must be abandoned... God creates by persuading the world to create itself... God proposes, the world disposes." [66]

And with reference to "risk" Ford wrote,—

> "The world is a risky affair for God as well as for us. God has taken

that risk upon himself in creating us with freedom through persuasion. He has faith in us, and it is up to us to respond in faith to him."[67]

It cannot be overemphasized that process theology is not Christian teaching. It is little more than ancient paganism with a finite, limited god, dressed in modern philosophical terminology. Yet, what did the process theologians say that the Arminians didn't? Rice and Pinnock denied that God exists outside of time; they denied that God has all knowledge of future events, they asserted that God is changeable and changing, and they asserted that God was taking "risks" in the world. Hartshorne and Ford denied that God exists outside of time; they denied that God has all knowledge of future events; they asserted that God is changing and progressing, and they asserted that God is taking risks in His relationship with the world and the future. What is the difference? Sure, we're aware that there are nuances of difference— Pinnock and Rice attempt to assert that God is not *ontologically dependent* upon the world while Hartshorne and Ford do not— but this point is not important enough to obscure the simple fact that true Arminians have no real basis for rejecting the main tenets of process theology! Isn't it therefore clear that the consistent Arminian is on a steep slippery slope that leads directly to the abyss called *finite godism*? There simply is no "stopping-off place" on the road to process theology for true, consistent Arminians. There are no convenient bushes at the edge of the cliff that the Arminian can grab on to just before he plunges over the edge into a system that is, in reality, little more than *philosophical atheism*.

Before we contrast the incredible statements above with the teaching of the Word of God below, we must once again insist that we are *not* saying that every Arminian denies the truth about God that is found throughout Scripture. We know many who do not accept the doctrines of grace, but who speak much of the sovereignty of God and His eternal nature and immutability. Our point here is this: such a person is living in inconsistency with his or her own beliefs. Arminianism leads to a denial of Christian theism as a necessity, for it is primarily based upon a limitation of the Creator for the sake of some mythical creaturely autonomy.

We shall now turn our attention to God's Word and one of the most richest passages in all of Scripture, Isaiah 40-45.

The Theology of God in Isaiah 40-45

Few books in the Old Testament provide a richer depth of theological knowledge than the wonderful prophecy of Isaiah ben Amoz.

The purpose of this study is to apply sound exegetical principles to the text of Isaiah 40-45 with the specific purpose of gleaning from this section an understanding of Isaiah's theology of God, and, by extension, the entire Bible's teaching of God. Tangent issues, such as textual variation or lexical problems, will be dealt with only in the context of their bearing on the theology presented here.

Isaiah 40-45 is clearly a literary whole; recurring themes, topics and phrases show this to be true. Some have titled this section the "Trial of the False Gods" in line with the judicial language found in 41:21 and elsewhere. Here Yahweh calls the idols to judgment and challenges them to a "battle of the gods." Of course, there is no reply forthcoming from the idols who are, by definition, silent. But in challenging the idolatry of the people of Israel, Yahweh reveals things about His nature and His purpose in the world that stand unparalleled in the Old Testament, and that is not in any way eclipsed by even the highest revelation of the New.

Historically, this section from Isaiah has held great importance to the Christian Church in the formulation of her doctrine of God. Few old Testament passages can claim any more foundational effect upon the beliefs of the Reformers in reference to God's sovereignty and providence than this one! As this writer comes from a Reformed perspective, it is admitted from the start that these passages lie dear to my heart. And, as we are concerned with examining the position being taken by modern exponents of Arminianism, which seriously challenges the Christian understanding of the doctrine of God itself, these ancient texts take on even more relevance in our modern situation!

The format of this inquiry into Isaiah's revelation of God's nature and purpose is simple. Sections of the text will be included, taken from the *New International Version* of the Bible. However, the custom of the NIV and other English translations in rendering the Tetragrammaton has altered in these citations. Given the importance of the name "Yahweh" to the revelation of God's being and His eternal purposes in covenant with Israel, the NIV's rendering of "LORD" has been replaced with the actual term "Yahweh." The text will be broken down thematically, and the main purpose of the section determined. From this material conclusions will be drawn in reference to the theology of God that is either directly asserted by the text, or which underlies the actions and words of God in the text.

Isaiah 40:12-17

Who has measured the waters in the hollow of his hand,
    or with the breadth of his hand marked off the heavens?
Who has held the dust of the earth in a basket, or weighed
    the mountains on the scales and the hills in a balance?
Who has understood the mind of Yahweh, or instructed him
    as his counselor?
Whom did Yahweh consult to enlighten him and who taught
    him the right way?
Who was it that taught him knowledge or showed him the
    path of understanding?
Surely the nations are like a drop in a bucket; they are
    regarded as dust on the scales; he weighs the islands as
    though they were fine dust.
Lebanon is not sufficient for altar fires, nor its animals
    enough for burnt offerings.

> *Before him all the nations are as nothing; they are regarded*
> *by him as worthless and less than nothing.*

This section follows a tender representation of Yahweh as shepherd of Israel (40:11); but even this is preceded by the assertion of the power and sovereignty of Yahweh in verse 10. Almost as a sudden thought, the writer begins a series of unanswerable rhetorical questions, designed to demonstrate the foolishness of questioning the capability of Yahweh to be faithful to Israel. The awesomeness of the Creator is here asserted by comparing Him to that which He has created. The great seas are seen as fitting into the palm of Yahweh's hand; the heavens themselves are defined by the size of His hand. The anthropomorphic language only heightens the "otherness" of Yahweh against that which He has created. The entire mass of the earth is called dust that God carries in a basket, or weighs upon scales as a merchant would weigh beans or produce. This is not a God who is intimidated by the tasks before Him!

Verses 13 and 14 speak of the impossibility of Yahweh's being taught by man, or learning anything from man. The rhetorical question is left unanswered, for there is no possibility of reply. God has never "learned" anything, for He is omniscient. No man can know the mind, or, literally, the "spirit" (Hb: *ruach*) of Yahweh. God is utterly independent and central in regards to knowledge and understanding. This is not a growing, progressing God, but an eternally complete and perfect God (in direct contradiction to process theology, and, as I have asserted, consistent, concluded Arminianism as seen in Rice and Pinnock).

Verses 15-17 take the assertions given by the questions of 12-14 and bring out the obvious conclusion— there is a great insufficiency in the created order to even begin to offer a sacrifice truly worthy of this God. Surely, only God's condescending grace allows for man's existence at all. God is surely not impressed by nations or kings, for they are "worthless" and "less than nothing." This is no geographically limited, politically controlled deity.

This passage sounds themes that will recur again and again in the following chapters. The author will stretch the reader to new heights in attempting to utilize human language to describe that which is completely other— Yahweh, King of Israel. In this passage the centrality of God to all knowledge— the cornerstone of epistemology (how we know what is true)— is clearly presented. God is not in need of man's wisdom or learning. God is not progressing in His knowledge of the world and man's actions. He is independent of the created order— transcendent, yet immanent in His providence.

Isaiah 40:18-20

> *To whom, then, will you compare God?*
> *What image will you compare him to?*
> *As for an idol, a craftsman casts it, and a goldsmith*
>   *overlays it with gold and fashions silver chains for it.*
> *A man too poor to present such an offering selects*
>   *wood that will not rot.*
> *He looks for a skilled craftsman to set up*
>   *an idol that will not topple.*

This section introduces another major theme for Isaiah— the impossibility of comparing Yahweh to anyone or anything else, and the foolishness of idolatry. It is assumed that in these passages Isaiah is most definitely engaging in deep, dreadfully truthful sarcasm in reference to idols and the construction of false gods. As God Himself is quoted as laying down these kinds of challenges, it is felt that the prophet would do the same.

In verse 18 Isaiah presents the *uniqueness* of Yahweh. One of the struggles of mankind is the fact that we learn by comparison. We define things by saying, "well, its *like* this...." But we cannot do this with God. God is unique. God is totally "other." We cannot compare Him to anything else, for to do so is to actually border on idolatry! There is nothing in the created order that is analogous to God. Every example will break down. God is infinite and uncreated— the universe is finite and created, and those attributes are carried into the very fabric of each and every thing in that universe. Hence, we cannot compare God to anything at all (see also Isaiah 46:5).

The Hebrew terms rendered "compare" in the first clause, and "image" in the second clause, both come from the Hebrew term *damut* which interestingly is the second of the terms used in Genesis 1:26 to define the relationship of man to God creatively. The first term *tselem* is normally translated "image" in Genesis 1:26, and this phrase as "likeness." There is a close connection between the Genesis creation language and the terminology and thoughts found here in Isaiah, and this connection will come up again in future passages.

Verses 19 and 20 make a very insightful comment into the nature of the human heart in idolatry. Whether the idol is the property of a rich man (vs. 19) or a poor man (vs. 20) it is still the same— an idol. And one's economic situation is irrelevant to the fact that man refuses to worship the one true God, but instead fashions idols, even if those idols differ in kind, size, shape, or expense (Romans 1:22-25!). Surely the Reformed view of anthropology is informed by passages such as this.

Isaiah 40:21-26

Do you not know?
Have you not heard?
Has it not been told you from the beginning?
Have you not understood since the earth was founded?
He sits enthroned above the circle of the earth,
*   and its people are like grasshoppers.*
He stretches out the heavens like a canopy,
*   and spreads them out like a tent to live in.*
He brings princes to naught and reduces
*   the rulers of this world to nothing.*
No sooner are they planted, no sooner are they sown,
*   no sooner do they take root in the ground,*
*   than he blows on them and they wither,*
*   and a whirlwind sweeps them away like chaff.*

"To whom will you compare me?
Or who is my equal?" says the Holy One.
Lift your eyes and look to the heavens:
Who created all these?
He who brings out the starry host one by one,
*   and calls them each by name.*
Because of his great power and mighty strength,
*   not one of them is missing.*

The question of verse 21 will reappear in 40:28. Here the sovereignty and providence of God is asserted to be a universal truth, and to be in the realm of universal knowledge. It is assumed that such a fact— the fact of God's awesomeness— has been known from the beginning, from before the very earth was founded! Here again is language and thinking that is basic to Pauline theology in Romans 1, especially verses 19 and 20.

God is pictured as sitting above the "circle of the earth," a rather unusual phrase possibly referring to the horizon, or maybe to the *rachia* ("firmament") of Genesis 1. Human beings are, in comparison to God, considered to be as grasshoppers. The heavens are pictured as subject to the plan and pleasure of Yahweh.

In verses 23-24, however, this great transcendence is again balanced by the direct assertion of providence. God is credited with working in history. He is concerned and involved in the affairs of men. Despite men's best plans, and despite the appearances of being invincible and strong (being "firmly planted"), Yahweh simply blows on them and they whither and are gone— no sign of them is left.

None of the local "gods" to whom the people of Israel are continuously bowing down can make such a claim as this. Their power and might is limited to their own particular geographical locality. Yet in light of God's actions in history, He asks His people again, "To whom will you compare me?" Who is God's equal?

To answer this question, Yahweh instructs his people to look at the stars above. Are these stars (which were worshipped by many of the local peoples at the time) deities? No, they are created objects, created and controlled by Yahweh Himself. They are upheld by "His great power and strength." Again creatorship and continued providence are asserted as clear and incontrovertible evidence of the absolute deity of Yahweh. Genesis language is used here again, for God is active in creating (Hb: *bara*) just as in the beginning. The heavens to which we are encouraged to look, however, are not described in the same language as in Genesis, but the concept is the same.

Isaiah 40:28-31

Do you not know? Have you not heard?
Yahweh is the everlasting God,
*   the Creator of the ends of the earth.*
He will not grow tired or weary,
*   and his understanding no one can fathom.*
He gives strength to the weary
*   and increases the power of the weak.*
Even youths grow tired and weary,
*   and young men stumble and fall;*
But those who hope in Yahweh
*   will renew their strength.*
They will soar on wings like eagles;
*   they will run and not grow weary,*
*   they will walk and not be faint.*

This section starts off with the same appeal to the common knowledge of man in regards to the true nature of God as was seen above. A literal translation of the second line of verse 28 might be, "A God eternal (is) Yahweh." Here eternity is connected with the concept of being Creator. The appeal that follows is based upon the nature of Yahweh. The text asserts the eternality of God, the creatorship of God, the omnipotence of God, and the omniscience of God. The verses that follow will base their promise of God's giving of strength to the "worm Jacob," the "little Israel" (Isaiah 41:14) on these attributes of His being.

The phrase "and his understanding no one can fathom" presents us with some unusual thoughts. The term *t*evonah* that is used here is not just "understanding" but is defined as "the object of knowledge." Man is incapable of examining or fathoming or understanding the storehouse of God's knowledge. Many reasons could be put forward as to why this is— His knowledge is infinite, and man is finite. We would not be out of line, given what has already been said by the prophet, to also allow the sense of eternality to enter into the discussion. God's knowledge is immediate and simultaneous— God does not, as seen above, grow in knowledge or experience, but, being eternal, experiences all points in time in a completely different manner than the creation man. It is important to remember that time is a creation-oriented thing; it is improper to attempt to limit God to existence within time, even if that time is infinitely extended. It is recognized that to think that someone as "primitive" as Isaiah could seriously be thought to have such lofty concepts in mind is extraordinary. But this writer not only believes that such a view misunderstands the nature of divine revelation, but such a view does injustice to ancient man, and to Isaiah in particular, by assuming a rather snobbish modern superiority and "enlightenment." It may just be that it is modern man, not ancient Isaiah, that has lost sight of the majesty and eternality of God.

This eternal and omnipotent God is not left in the realm of the untouchable and disconnected; rather, Yahweh is seen here again as graciously functioning as the covenant God of Israel, granting to them strength and power. This power is given to those who "wait" upon Yahweh— the term, by extension, can properly refer to "trust," for faithfulness is measured over the long term in Hebrew thought. God's promise is that He will grant supernatural strength in patient endurance that is of a different kind than the natural strength of the youthful or the strong.

Isaiah 41:1-4

"Be silent before me, you islands!
Let the nations renew their strength!
Let them come forward and speak;
*   let us meet together at the place of judgment.*
"Who has stirred up one from the east,

calling him in righteousness to his service?
He hands nations over to him and
  subdues kings before him.
He turns them to dust with his sword,
  to wind-blown chaff with his bow.
He pursues them and moves on unscathed,
  by a path his feet have not traveled before.
Who has done this and carried it through,
  calling forth the generations from the beginning?
I, Yahweh— with the first of them and
  with the last— I am he."

Here we enter into the "trial" narrative itself. Yahweh uses the language of the courtroom to prosecute those "gods" who would call for the worship of His people Israel. In this segment God's actions in history— primarily the calling of Cyrus to defeat the Babylonians and free the remnant from captivity— is submitted as evidence of God's rulership of the universe. A passage such as this would be cited as evidence of a later date for this section, given the presupposition that there is no prophetic ability to speak futuristically. The language, admittedly, gives weight upon first reading to a past event. But this is to be interpreted as a futuristic usage in prophetic language.

The first verse summons the nations to judgment. In verses 2 and 3 reference is made to the awesome power and might of Cyrus, whom God is said to have "stirred up from the east." Cyrus is seen as serving God in righteousness, though this is not to be taken in a personal way in regards to the man himself. Here the meaning would lean toward the understanding of "fulfilling God's purpose" rather than any kind of moral or ethical understanding. Cyrus' success is directly attributed to the work of Yahweh for His people (compare 40:23-24).

These actions are described in verse 4 as being in conformity with the eternal purpose and will of God. The fact that God is capable of sovereignly bringing about the deliverance of His people is here seen as evidence of His true nature and divine power. Yahweh is seen as the source of time itself— the one who calls out "the generations from the beginning." Yahweh is then quoted as saying, "I, Yahweh— with the first of them and with the last— I am he." This phrase is laden with meaning. Of course, the term Yahweh itself is connected by many scholars with the eternal nature of God and His consistency in His actions within time. Yahweh is here said to be "with" the first "of them"— the "them" referring to the generations— and "with" the last of them as well. God's instantaneous and personal presence in all of time seems to be the direction of the thought at this point. Note also the usage of the term merosh— "from the beginning." This is again language similar to Genesis 1.

Isaiah 41:21-24

"Present your case," says Yahweh.
"Set forth your arguments," says Jacob's King.
"Bring in your idols to tell us what is going to happen.
Tell us what the former things were,
      so that we may consider them and
      know their full outcome.
Or declare to us the things to come,
      tell us what the future holds,
      so that we may know that you are gods.
Do something, whether good or bad,
      so that we will be dismayed and filled with fear.
But you are less than nothing and your works
      are utterly worthless; he who chooses you is detestable."

Yahweh now calls for the presentation of the case of the opposition. Those who oppose His kingship are invited to "set forth" their arguments. God doesn't mind the confrontation. He is true, and what He says is true, and hence it will be demonstrated to be the truth. He doesn't fear what men will say or do.

Verse 22 calls for the idols to be brought (they can't come themselves!) and to speak. What are they challenged to discuss? They are first challenged to "tell us what is going to happen." Yahweh knows the future and rules over it because He is the creator of it. Can the idol boast of this? No "god" is worthy of the name unless they meet this requirement. The second challenge is just as high. Can the idols "tell us what the former things were"? This is not just historical knowledge, but knowledge of purpose. Yahweh asks not just for a recitation of the bald facts of history, but the demonstration of the meaning behind those actions. Here we have an underlying thought that all that takes place in time is purposeful and meaningful, primarily because Yahweh is at work within time. This is not simply the result of theological reflection over long periods of time, finally codified at Westminster! No, Yahweh throws the gauntlet down to all who would pretend to be God— tell us what is going to happen, and tell us about what has happened and the purposes for which those actions took place! Certainly those who propose a "learning" God who is changing and learning are completely contradicted by such passages as this!

Isaiah's pen drips with sarcasm as God seems to plead with the idols to at least do *something* good or bad! One is reminded of Elijah on the mountain mocking the priests of Baal. "Is your God out at the bathroom?" he asks. Here Yahweh asks that the idols do something so that "we will be dismayed and filled with fear." But there is no response. So, in verse 24, God drops the sarcasm and speaks the truth: the idol is less than nothing, its works utterly worthless, and the one who is foolish enough to choose to bow down to this lifeless hunk of material is himself detestable.

Isaiah 42:5-9

This is what Yahweh God says—
He who created the heavens and stretched them out,
   who spread out the earth and all that comes out of it,
   who gives breath to its people,
   and life to those who walk on it:
"I, Yahweh, have called you in righteousness;
   I will take hold of your hand.
I will keep you and will make you
   to be a covenant for my people and a light
   for the Gentiles, to open eyes that are blind,

to set free captives from prison and to release
    from the dungeon those who sit in darkness.
"I am Yahweh; that is my name!
    I will not give my glory to another
    or my praise to idols.
See, the former things have taken place,
    and new things I declare;
    before they spring into being
    I announce them to you."

The pattern of Isaiah's oracles in this section should now be familiar. Before announcing the content of the next statement from God, Yahweh is described in terms that will have direct bearing on the nature of what is said. Here, in verse 5, Yahweh God is described in two couplets. The first is that He is the creator— He created the heavens, and He stretched them out. The second is that Yahweh is the giver of life itself. He gives breath to the people, life to those who walk on the earth. Clearly,— creation = stretching out; breath = life. It would seem to be wise then to listen closely to He who gives us our very breath; our very life! In verse 8 Yahweh proclaims, or makes known, His name (a fact sadly missed by most English translations!). Yahweh's name is glorious (Psalm 72:19), and because it represents His very nature and being, God is jealous of that name. He will not allow His glory to be given to another, or His praise to idols. It is fascinating that this proclamation of the jealousy of Yahweh for worship is followed immediately by a passage closely connected to the above discussions in chapter 41. God is worthy of praise and glory, and this is revealed again by His revelation of what has taken place, and His revelation of what is about to come to pass.

Isaiah 43:1-7

But now, this is what Yahweh says— he who created you,
    O Jacob, he who formed you, O Israel:
"Fear not, for I have redeemed you;
    I have summed you by name; you are mine.

When you pass through the waters,
   I will be with you; and when you pass through the rivers,
they will not sweep over you.
When you walk through the fire, you will not be burned;
   the flames will not set you ablaze.
For I am Yahweh, your God,
   the Holy One of Israel, your Savior;
I give Egypt for your ransom, Cush and Seba in your stead.
Since you are precious and honored in my sight,
   and because I love you,
   I will give men in exchange for you,
   and people in exchange for your life.
Do not be afraid, for I am with you;
   I will bring your children from the east
   and gather you from the west.
I will say to the north, 'Give them up!'
   and to the south, 'Do not hold them back.'
Bring my sons from afar and my daughters from
   the ends of the earth—
   everyone who is called by my name,
   whom I created for my glory,
   whom I formed and made."

In verse 1, Israel is seen to be the object of God's creative acts. Two terms are used here, *bara* and *yazar*. In Isaiah, these two terms are paralleled frequently. Yahweh is the creator of the universe, and, in a special and personal way, the creator of Israel. This is continued in verse 2 where redemption language comes into view— Yahweh has redeemed Israel, and has called Jacob by name. This personal summons reflects God's ownership and love for Israel that forms the centerpiece of this section (v. 4).

God's promise is not that Israel will not pass through the waters, or walk through the fire. God does not remove His people from living in a fallen world. But the promise is to be with His people through these trials and ordeals. The phrase "I will be with you" is the first person way of saying *Immanuel!* He is the faithful covenant God of Israel.

God's love for Israel is seen in His willingness to give others for the ransom of Israel. Peoples are exchanged for the life of this small group who would seem to us to be insignificant from a human perspective. In verses 5 and 6 God's ability to restore Israel, no matter how severe the dispersion, is asserted. When one comes to verse 7, the same verbs are found as were seen in verse 1, though added here is the small, but immensely important thought— the purpose of God in creating His chosen people is for His own glory. This thought is not new, as the above discussions have shown.

This section is a literary whole. The first three verses of the unit lead up to verse 4 and God's proclamation of His love for Israel. Then the same steps are retraced through verses 5-7, only in reverse order so that verse 1 is parallel to verse 7, etc.

Isaiah 43:10-13

> "You are my witnesses," declares Yahweh,
>   "and my servant whom I have chosen,
>   so that you may know and believe me
>   and understand that I am he.
> Before me no god was formed,
>   nor will there be one after me.
> I, even I, am Yahweh,
>   and apart from me there is no savior.
> I have revealed and saved and proclaimed—
>   I, and not some foreign god among you.
> You are my witnesses," declares Yahweh, "that I am God.
> Yes, and from ancient days I am he.
> No one can deliver out of my hand.
> When I act, who can reverse it?"

The law-court language continues with the summons of Israel to the witness stand. Yahweh claims that Israel is his chosen servant with the purpose that they should know Him, and believe Him (*yada* and *aman*). Here again this phrase is used in parallel with Yahweh, and as a definition thereof. It is followed immediately by radical monotheism— the single strongest statement (in my opinion) of monotheism in Scripture. Especially striking is the fact that Jesus uses almost identical language in John 13:19 (The Septuagint is nearly word-for-word with Jesus), and in John's gospel Jesus uses the phrase in the context of revealing future events, an action that is clearly connected with Yahweh in these passages. It seems unavoidable that there is a proper connection here, and that in fact the usage of *ego eimi* by Jesus in John 13:19 finds its foundation here in Isaiah's use of *ani hu*.

Verse 11 claims that Yahweh Himself is the only savior— the only hope for Israel. There is no other savior— no other foreign god who can deliver Israel, who can declare to them what is to come! God appeals to their common sense. They are His witnesses. Their testimony must surely be that Yahweh, not some other god, is the one who is at work with them. They are witnesses precisely because they are the objects of the actions enumerated in this passage— God has revealed Himself to them; He has saved or redeemed them; He has proclaimed to them His will and His name.

This is not a new situation. Yahweh has eternally been the same. Even from eternity Yahweh has been the "I am." Here again *ani hu* is used in the same senses as before. His actions have always been sovereign, just as they are now. When Yahweh acts, is there anyone who can (literally) "turn it back"? Since no answer is given, the answer is sure— nothing in the created order can override the sovereign decree of God. This is both a comfort and a reason to fear. It is a comfort for those who seek God's glory and who accept all from His hand. It is a fear for those who arrogantly attempt to set themselves up in His place, and grab for themselves some sort of personal sovereignty. Such is a reversal of the created order, and Yahweh will not stand for it.

Isaiah 44:6-8

"This is what Yahweh says—
Israel's King and Redeemer Yahweh Almighty:
I am the first and I am the last;

apart from me there is no God.
Who then is like me? Let him proclaim it.
  Let him declare and lay out before me
what has happened since I established my ancient people,
  and what is yet to come—
  yes, let him foretell what will come.
Do not tremble, do not be afraid.
  Did I not proclaim this and foretell it long ago?
You are my witnesses. Is there any God besides me?
  No, there is no other Rock; I know not one."

Isaiah 44:6-8 pulls together themes from many of the preceding sections and connects them together in a breathtaking proclamation of Yahweh's claims. Yahweh here says that He is *both* the first and the last. This differs from 41:4 where He was *with* the first and the last of the generations; here He is the first and the last, or, as the New Testament will express it, He is the beginning and the end. This is another of the ways Yahweh expresses in human language the absoluteness of His being. If He is first and last, then His is the ground of all else. His being cannot, therefore, be derivative or temporal in any way. He is first and last; He was not first, and will someday be last, but both are a present reality to God. Such knowledge is too high for the human mind! Our finite beings, limited as we are to the slavery of temporal existence, balk at such concepts as this! But, simply because we are in ourselves *insufficient* for such things is no basis for rejecting them as true![68]

Since God is eternal, it is self-evident that there are no other gods. Those who would make this claim are invited to respond to the same challenge laid down previously— let them make proclamation of the past and its purposes, primarily in reference to His "ancient people." And what is coming in the future?

The comforting words "do not be afraid" find an echo above in God's mocking of the idols, seeking from them some action that would cause fear and trembling. Since there is no action forthcoming, just as it is sure here that there is none other who knows the course of the future, there is no need to fear. Israel does not need to fear that her covenant God is going to abandon her. If there were indeed other gods in existence anywhere who could compare with Yahweh, then there would be no absolute assurance that these gods would not in some way affect the promises of Yahweh to the people of Israel. But no such possibility exists. Is there any other God besides Him? No, there is no other. He whose understanding and knowledge is infinite (Psalm 147:5) does not know of a single other god. Is it possible that He who stretched out the heavens by Himself (44:24) would not know of another God, if such a God existed? Certainly not.

Isaiah 44:24-26:

"This is what Yahweh says—
  your Redeemer, who formed you in the womb:
I am Yahweh, who has made all things,
  who alone stretched out the heavens,
  who spread out the earth by myself,
  who foils the signs of false prophets
and makes fools of diviners
  who overthrows the learning of the wise
and turns it to nonsense,
  who carries out the words of his servants
  and fulfills the predictions of his messengers."

The intensely personal relationship of Yahweh to Israel, seen before, is here expressed in familiar language. Here Yahweh claims to be the very one who formed Israel in the womb. Here is creation par excellence! The now customary catalog of attributes is then introduced. As if repetition will cause our dull minds to fully grasp the significance of it, the Holy Word again tells us that Yahweh is creator, Yahweh made all things. But the Lord goes beyond this to make it so emphatic as to establish the fact forever: Yahweh alone stretched out the heavens— He needed no help, had no company. He *alone* spread out the earth. If Yahweh did all this, then where could these other gods live?

They would have to partake of the created order themselves, and hence be subject to Yahweh. No stone is left unturned in God's quest to express the simple fact that there is no other god— anywhere— beside Him.

However, as the Word is careful to do, balance is maintained. God not only hung the stars in the sky, but He is active in the world as well. Here His activity is that of bringing to naught the predictions of the "diviners" and the words of the false prophets. It is not that those who represent the idols will keep silent as the idol does! No, men, without hearing even from their own dumb idol, will speak presumptuously, and God says He delights in making them look foolish (1 Kings 22:22-23). They have no real knowledge of what God is doing in the world. They cannot help but look silly when reality shows them to be fools. But, not so with the true servants of God! God is described here as the one who "carries out the words of his servants." This is not to say that these servants give messages that they did not receive from God. Rather, Yahweh "fulfills the predictions of His messengers." As long as the prophet is acting as the messenger and not the author, God will be with him! Certainly men such as Amos or Jeremiah could find solace in such a promise, in such a description of their God. The whole passage is reminiscent of Deuteronomy 18.

Isaiah 45:4-7:

> "For the sake of Jacob my servant, of Israel my chosen,
> I summon you by name and bestow on you a title of honor,
>   though you do not acknowledge me.
> I am Yahweh, and there is no other;
>   apart from me there is no God.
> I will strengthen you, though you have not acknowledged me,
>   so that from the rising of the sun to the place of its setting
>   men may know there is none besides me.
> I am Yahweh, and there is no other.

> *I form light and create darkness,*
> *I bring prosperity and create disaster;*
>   *I, Yahweh, do all these things."*

Verse 4 opens with the Hebrew term *l^ema'an* translated "for the sake of." Here this term refers to God's covenant loyalty and love for Jacob. Israel is His "chosen" people. Because of this, God calls them by name (see above) and gives to Israel a title of honor, and this fully of grace, for they do not even acknowledge Him! Literally the term is *yadah*, a Hebrew term used frequently in these passages and capable of many nuances of meaning. In 44:8 God is said not to "know" of any other gods; clearly there it is not simply "acknowledge" that is meant, but a flat denial of the existence of such beings. Here we may allow for a simple lack of acknowledgment on Israel's part, but in practicality could this not refer to a denial of Yahweh based on idolatry? It certainly is a possibility. Hosea will cry out, "There is no knowledge of God in the land!" Hosea 4:1. This could be Yahweh's charge here as well.

So why does God remain faithful? Certainly it is His character to do so, but the specific purpose brought into play here has to do with the proclamation of this fact: *"I am Yahweh, and there is no other."* This is repeated twice in this section of the text. God will strengthen Israel to show His own glory, just as He raised up Pharaoh for the same purpose.

Verse 7 stretches the human willingness to accept God's revelation of Himself. It is not as if this verse were all alone— the entire Scriptural witness confirms that these words are true. But that does not make things any easier. When Yahweh commissioned Moses to go to Pharaoh, He informed Moses that He was the one who made man's mouth, who makes man deaf or mute, who gives him sight or makes him blind (Exodus 4:11). So Yahweh's words here are certainly not without precedent.

Yahweh says He forms[69] light, and creates[70] darkness; then, the Hebrew literally reads, "I am making peace (*shalom*) and creating evil (*ra*)." Just how *ra* is to be taken here is difficult to say. Whatever it is, whether "evil," "calamity," or "disaster," it is just as much the opposite of *shalom* as light is the opposite of darkness in the preceding clause. Those who wish to escape God's sovereignty and the related problem of "theodicy" (the problem of evil) find no escape here, even by opting for a "softer" translation, for the simple fact of the matter is that God is claiming responsibility for actions in time. Both actions which can be described as "peaceful," and those which cannot, come from the one hand of God. Certainly the Reformed concept of providence finds a source in an affirmation such as this.

Isaiah 45:9-10:

> "Woe to him who quarrels with his Maker,
>   to him who is but a potsherd among
>   the potsherds on the ground.
> Does the clay say to the potter,
>   'What are you making?'
> Does your work say,
>   'He has no hands?'
> Woe to him who says to his father,
>   'What have you begotten?'
> or to his mother,
>   'What have you brought to birth?' "

Following hard on the heels of the many and repetitive statements of the sovereignty of Yahweh over the universe, this passage again gives insight into the foolishness of attitudes that are so frequently a part of human existence that only by being dazzled by the brightness of the glory of God are we able to then plainly see the foolishness of our own thoughts and actions. Here is language that fits in Romans 9. Woe to the man who quarrels with his Maker! Indeed! The examples given are in reality humorous, but they don't read that way given man's forgetfulness of his own created status! Man is said to be a "potsherd among the potsherds on the ground." He is just a broken fragment left in the dust. What does he have to complain about? And does the clay speak up and inquire as to the purposes of the potter? Does a pot deny that it was fashioned by the hands of its maker? Certainly not! Yet this is exactly what man does with Yahweh. The analogy continues on using the parent/child relationship. No one would deny that he was begotten by his mother and father— yet Israel will not acknowledge his maker, the one who "formed" him in the womb (44:24)!

Isaiah 45:18-19:

> *For this is what Yahweh says—*
>   *he who created the heavens, he is God;*
> *he who fashioned and made the earth, he founded it;*
> *he did not create it to be empty,*
>   *but formed it to be inhabited—*
> *he says:*
> *"I am Yahweh, and there is no other.*
> *I have not spoken in secret,*
>   *from somewhere in a land of darkness;*
> *I have not said to Jacob's descendants,*
>   *'Seek me in vain.'*
> *I, Yahweh, speak the truth;*
>   *I declare what is right."*

Another oracle is here introduced with the repeated assertion of creatorship. An addition is here made, however. We are told that Yahweh did not create the world "to be empty." Here again is Genesis creation narrative language, for the term here is *tohu,* the exact same word used in Genesis 1:2 where the earth is *tohu wa'bohu*— without form, and empty. The explicit claim is made that this is not part of the purpose of God. But interestingly the same word will be used by Yahweh in verse 19 when He denies that He has ever said to Jacob's descendants, "seek me in vain" (*tohu*). Also, another creation prologue word shows up here— *hoshek* describes the land of darkness in verse 19.

Yahweh here denies that He had not revealed Himself sufficiently to Jacob. Certainly their entire history gives affirmation to Yahweh's words! Not only this, but Yahweh *is speaking* (participle in the Hebrew) that which the NIV translates as "truth." It is the Hebrew term *tsedek*— that which is right, hence, by extension, that which is true. Anything that is in right relationship to the Creator is true; indeed, without the absolute of the Creator, there can be no such thing as truth, for Yahweh defines truth. Yahweh makes known, this passage says, what is true and what is right. Israel cannot make the excuse of ignorance.

Isaiah 45:21-23:

"Declare what is to be, present it—
   let them take counsel together.
Who foretold this long ago,
   who declared it from the distant past?
Was it not I, Yahweh? And there is no God apart from me,
   a righteous God and a Savior; there is none but me.
Turn to me and be saved, all you ends of the earth;
   for I am God, and there is no other.
By myself I have sworn,
   my mouth has uttered in all integrity
   a word that will not be revoked:
Before me every knee will bow;
   by me every tongue will swear."

This section ties together themes and phrases that we have now seen repeated over and over again. Verse 21 lays down the challenge again— Yahweh, and Yahweh alone, makes known the future. He alone controls what takes place in time. This fact alone demonstrates that there are none others like Him. He alone is God. There are no gods other than He.

This magnificent, powerful, omniscient and eternal God, miracle of all miracles, proclaims Himself to be "a righteous God and a Savior." Given the potsherd passage above, one can see just how false is the idea that grace is a solely New Testament term! Because God is Savior, He invites not just Israel, but all the ends of the earth to come to Him and be saved. He is the sole source of refuge. Yahweh goes against modern trends— Yahweh will have nothing of "comparative religions"— Yahweh is the sole source of salvation. One cannot find salvation anywhere but in Him.

Every knee will bow to Yahweh. This promise is as sure as any that can be made. God has promised. The word has gone forth "in all integrity." This promise cannot be revoked. Every knee, sometime, someway, will bow to Him. Every tongue will confess His name. Given this, can we avoid amazement at the quotation of this passage in Philippians 2:10-11? For Paul, this promise will be fulfilled when all acknowledge Jesus Christ as *Kurios* (can we not say *Yahweh?*), resulting in the glorification of the Father.

Conclusions

There comes a point, in reading and thinking over these passages, when the mind becomes numb at the majesty of the Person who here graciously reveals Himself to the creature man. One is struck at the fact that such revelation is completely a gift of grace.

At the same time, the issues here discussed are of such a profoundly basic nature that one is tempted to miss them. Our Creator clearly tells us that if we are to function as He has designed us to function, we must acknowledge Him not in any form we wish to, but as He truly is. God requires of us faith in Him as He exists, not as we would like to re-shape and reform Him into our image and likeness.

God stresses in these passages His role as creator. Nearly every section examined contained this truth, and built upon it the claims of God upon Israel as well as the basis for their being able to trust in Him. A corollary of this is Yahweh's eternal nature. This God does not exist within time, subservient to it, but He is the creator of time, the one who declares what has happened and what will happen in the future. God's existence in eternity is part of that which makes Him wholly "other" than finite, temporal man.

Since God is creator and eternal, there obviously can be no other gods besides Him. Here is a reasoned defense of monotheism. Polytheism is self-contradictory and foolish. It denies the very nature of the created universe, and the nature of Yahweh as He has revealed Himself. Polytheism, no matter what form these "gods" might take, is simple idolatry. A god who is not like Yahweh— who is not eternal and omniscient and sovereign— is no god at all, and those who would choose such a god are, the Scripture says, *detestable.*

Finally, can a greater contrast be found than the one between the clear teachings of Scripture, and the citations found at the beginning of this appendix from Arminians and process theologians? If one wishes to be an Arminian, a consistent, thoroughgoing denier of the doctrines of grace, then one should find an edition of the Bible that does not have Isaiah's writings in its table of contents!

12

Appendix C

Answers to a Few Common Objections

In this section we will provide short, basic answers to some of the most common objections that are raised against the Reformed perspective. The listing of questions is purposefully short, as are the answers. I do not believe that these answers will convince anyone who is looking for reasons *not* to believe. But they will provide help for those seeking a consistent understanding of the issues.

Q. *2 Peter 3:9 indicates that God does not want anyone to perish. Doesn't this disprove the doctrine of election?*

A. We must always apply sound rules of exegesis to the Scriptures. Peter accepted the Old Testament's teaching about the nature of God. He knew Psalm 135:6 and Psalm 115:3, and the truth that whatever God pleases, He does. And, since we have already seen that repentance is the gift of God, could He not give repentance to anyone He chooses? Finally, the context of the passage must be consulted. 2 Peter is written to the elect, as 2 Peter 1:1 shows. In chapter 3, Peter is explaining the delay of the *parousia*, that is, the coming of Christ. He explains that Christ will indeed return, and that the delay is in order that God may gather His people. "He is patient with you," Peter writes to God's people, "not wanting anyone to perish, but everyone to come to repentance." The "everyone" is in reference to all of God's elect. The only reason that you are reading this book nearly 2,000 years later is because God has been patient, giving the world all this time, so that all of God's elect could be gathered in.

Q. *1 Timothy 2:4 says that God wants all men to be saved and to come to a knowledge of the truth. Doesn't this disprove the concept of election?*

A. Again, the entire context of Scripture, as well as of this passage, must be considered. Aside from all the passages that clearly indicate God's ability to save all men and bring everyone to a knowledge of the truth if He so desired, we again note the context of 1 Timothy 2:5 which speaks of the mediatorship of Christ, and as we saw in our examination of the atonement and intercession of Christ, this work is undertaken on behalf of God's people. Therefore, the term "men" in verse 5 is limited to the elect of God. As John Owen noted in this regard,—

> What then, I pray? what will be concluded hence? Cannot Christ be a mediator between God and men, but he must be a mediator for all men? Are not the elect men? do not the children partake of flesh and blood? doth not his church consist of men? What reason is there to assert, out of an indefinite proposition, a universal conclusion? Because Christ was a mediator for men (which were true had he been so only for his apostles), shall we conclude therefore he was so for all men?[71]

The same is to be said for verse 6, where the ransom sacrifice of Christ is mentioned. We have seen that this sacrifice was made in behalf of the people of God, not for each and every individual. Therefore, if verses five and six specifically mention the work of Christ in behalf of the elect, verse four does as well. This fits consistently with the entire teaching of Scripture. "All men" here is the same "all" that are given by the Father to the Son in John 6:37.

Q. *Doesn't the Bible exhort "whosoever will" to come?*

A. Yes, it does. The Gospel message is addressed to all men. However, just who "wills" to come? We know that the natural man does not understand the things of the Spirit of God (1 Corinthians 2:14) and that no man seeks after God (Romans 3:11). We also know that the Lord Jesus said that no man is *able* to come to Him unless the Father draws him (John 6:44). So, outside of God's initial move in regeneration, no man will "will" to come to Christ.

Q. *If God has already chosen who will be saved, why share the gospel, since they will be saved whether we are involved in evangelism or not?*

A. This is probably the most common objection that is voiced against the doctrine of election. There is a clear answer, but before getting to that, we should note that the question is not a proper one; that is, our questions should be based upon the teaching of the word of God, not what we can or cannot necessarily understand. Even if *we* did not have an answer to the question, would this necessarily mean that Ephesians 1:11 does not teach what it obviously teaches?

We do have an answer though. First, we evangelize to glorify God. We do not go out to "save" anybody, since we are incapable of doing that in the first place. We share the gospel because by so doing, we bring glory to God. If that is all the reason we had, it would be sufficient.

Yet there is more. We know that God has given us a great *privilege* to be used by Him in His work in this world. He has given us a blessing to be able to share the gospel with men. God has decreed both the ends *and* the means. He has decreed to use men in sharing the gospel with His elect. Why has He done so? I don't fully know. I only know that His Word reveals it to be so.

God has not seen fit to give us knowledge of who is, and who is not, His elect. Therefore, we share the gospel with *all* men, and trust God to honor the proclamation of His message by draw-ing the elect unto Himself. We can share boldly with all men, knowing that God is powerful to save, and as long as we seek to glorify Him, He will care for us and bless us with His Spirit.

Q. *But doesn't the"Calvinistic" view of God characterize man as nothing but a puppet or a robot?*

A. While this is often asserted, I have found few who have thought through their question. What is really being said is that a sovereign God cannot produce living, responsible beings (like man). Unless man himself is *autonomous*, that is, absolutely free to determine his own destiny, then he is not free, but is simply a puppet or a robot. But why is this? Why can God not remain sovereign and create man in His image? There are many things that God is that we are not— God is eternal, we are not; God is omniscient, we are not; so, if God is sovereign, why must we be autonomous?

The Bible tells us that God loves us, and has sent His Son to die in our place. We have been united with Christ, and we have a relationship with God through Him. Christ does not die for puppets. His blood was not shed for robots. Automatons do not enter into personal relationships.

What we really see in this question is a common, human as-sertion: if God's truth cannot be easily understood by the hu-man mind, then it must not be true. Is it necessary that God reveal how He could create us as responsible beings and yet remain the sole sovereign of the universe?

Q. *Do you expect me to believe in a God who would force people to be saved?*

A. I don't believe in such a God. Dead men have no ability to resist the sovereign grace of God, so how can the word "force" have any meaning? To "force" someone assumes that they are able to resist. God never forces anyone to do anything against their "will," for those who are left in their sin are enslaved to evil and do not desire to follow after God. Those whom God regenerates are made new creatures by His work, and therefore desire His will, His purpose. They are no more "forced" to be saved than Lazarus was "forced" to come out of the tomb.

Q. *Doesn't Galatians 5:4; and Hebrews 6:4-6 teach that we can lose our salvation?*

A. Galatians 5:4 is written to those who attempt to be justified by their own works. They thereby refuse God's grace, God's way of righteousness. It is because of this that they are said to be severed from Christ, and to have "fallen" from grace, but *these men were not Christians to begin with.*

There are a number of passages in Hebrews that provide "warnings" to the Church. In each instance, the entire Christian fellowship is addressed. The book of Hebrews is written to all who are a part of that fellowship— *including* non-believers, some of whom were not completely convinced of the superiority of Christ over the old law, others who were simply hypocrites. The warnings that are provided are needed since we, as human beings, cannot see into the hearts of all men. We cannot assume, simply because someone sits in the pew next to us each Sunday, that they are of God's elect. The minister of God's people must exhort his people to examine their lives— knowing that some who sit before him are not actually followers of Jesus Christ.

However, are we justified, in light of all the plain Scriptures affirming the security of the believer, to take warning passages to the Church and use them to deny that Christ will save His people? Are warning passages sufficient basis to assert that Christ can fail to do the will of the Father? Is this consistent biblical interpretation? I think not.

Endnotes

[1] Certainly we know that Jesus Christ, the Second Person of the Trinity, became flesh and entered into human existence. But prior to the incarnation, God revealed the truth about His eternal existence, and His uniqueness and difference from man is part and parcel of that revelation.

[2] Or, that time has priority to God in the sense that God is limited to the parameters set upon Him by time, rather than time being limited by the creative decree of God.

[3] We note as well that Yahweh uses the Hebrew phrase here, *ani hu*. This phrase is translated in the Septuagint as (greek font) egw eim. John uses this phrase of Christ in many places (John 8:24, 58, 18:5-6) and quite significantly in the same context of the revelation of future events (as here in 41:4) in John 13:19. See discussion of these passages in Appendix B.

[4] See Appendix B for further information on this concept.

[5] John Calvin, Institutes of the Christian Religion, ed. by John T. McNeill (Westminster Press, Philadelphia, 1960), I:13:1, p. 121.

[6] Ibid.I:17:13, p. 227.

[7] See also Psalm 10:16, 47:7-8, Isaiah 6:5, Jeremiah 10:10, and 1 Timothy 6:15-16.

[8] We emphasize as well the words of the Psalmist in verse 8. All the peoples of the earth are to fear and revere God. This is the proper

attitude of all who recognize God's true being, His true nature as Creator and Sovereign.

[9] We note that there is much, much more that must be said about God. We do not omit His mercy, His grace, His love, His kindness, etc. These truths will be self-evident as we examine His grace toward mankind. But these truths have been badly misunderstood because God's nature as the eternal, sovereign Creator has been neglected. As we said above, God must be seen in His completeness, not in bits and pieces.

[10] Jonathan Edwards, "Sermon on Romans 9:18" in *The Works of Jonathan Edwards* (London: Banner of Truth Trust, 1974), II:854

[11] Ibid.

[12] Sin *results in* our denial of the sovereignty of God, as we shall see when we examine Romans 1.

[13] I am not here addressing the truth that man *from his creation*, even before the fall, has been dependent upon God's revelation.

[14] Calvin, *Institutes* I:2:2, pp. 37-38.

[15] Note that even repentance itself is something that must be given by God!

[16] As opposed to predestination, which is usually used for the entire concept of God's sovereign decree in all of creation. Election speaks specifically to salvation, and that of men. When we speak of "predestination and election" we are speaking of both the general sovereignty of God as well as the specific sovereignty of God in the salvation of men.

[17] For a discussion of the meaning of foreknowledge, see Appendix A.

[18] Romans 8:7.

[19] See Appendix A.

[20] This is another clear passage refuting the concept of election based upon foreknowledge of future actions on the part of man.

[21] Of course, we know that Pharaoh did not want to obey God in the first place. He was as much of a rebel as anyone else, and was not "forced" to do anything against his will. His heart was filled with evil, and God used him to accomplish His purposes, fully in line with the desires of Pharaoh's heart.

[21] Edwin H. Palmer, *The Five Points of Calvinism*, Grand Rapids: Baker Book House, 1980; pp. 41-55.

[22] Palmer, The Five Points of Calvinism, p. 47.

[23] Lorraine Boettner, *The Reformed Doctrine of Predestination*, Phillipsburg, New Jersey: Presbyterian and Reformed Publishing Com-

pany, 1932; p. 153.

[24] This passage is often used to *deny* the specific atonement of Christ; yet, when the parallel passage in John 11:51-52 is consulted, it is clear that John means the "world" to be taken in the same sense that is explained for us in Revelation 5:9-11, where Christ's death purchases for God men "from every tribe and language and people and nation," that is, from all the *world*.

[25] I am not in this chapter denying that the death of Christ had *effects* for all men, indeed, for all of creation. I believe that His death is indeed part of the "summing up of all things" in Christ. But, we are speaking here solely with the salvific effect of the *substitutionary* atonement of Christ. One might say that Christ's death has an *effect* upon those for whom it was not intended as an atoning sacrifice.

[26] The reader is strongly encouraged to make the effort to read completely a work that stands as a classic in the field: John Owen's *The Death of Death in the Death of Christ* from Banner of Truth, for a full discussion of the issues surrounding the atonement of Christ.

[27] John Owen, *The Death of Death in the Death of Christ*, London: Banner of Truth Trust, 1985) pp. 61-62.

[28] Obviously, those who attempt to make this "washing" equal to baptism are missing Paul's entire message of the God-centeredness of salvation.

[29] See also Paul's testimony to this truth in 1 Timothy 1:14.

[30] This is my personal translation of Romans 8:5-8; the NIV translates the term "flesh" as "sinful nature," which, though often an accurate understanding of the concept, is not strictly translation.

[31] Some attempt to say that there are those who are truly saved but are not of the elect. Aside from there being no Biblical support for such a position, what we have seen of man's deadness in sin, and his inability to come to Christ (John 6:44), refutes such a concept completely.

[32] Of course, such a unity in salvation can only come from the unity that is theirs in the Godhead.

[33] Such as the Waldensians, Albigenses, etc.

[34] Dr. Nathan Feldmeth, to whom I am tremendously indebted for dispelling the cloud of confusion about Church History, and for being used of God to instill in its place a deep love for that subject.

[35] Martin Luther, *The Bondage of the Will* (translator: Henry Cole, Grand Rapids: Baker Book House, 1976) p. 240, 242.

[36] Ibid, pp. 321-322.

[37] Ibid., p. 372.

[38] Ibid., p. 390.

[39] John Calvin, Institutes of the Christian Religion, (Philadelphia: Westminster Press, 1960) I:2:1, p. 41.

[40] Ibid., I:IV:1, p. 47.

[41] Ibid., I:XVI:3, p. 200.

[42] Ibid., II:II:12, pp. 270-271.

[43] See Appendix B for a discussion of this issue.

[44] Calvin, Institutes III:21:1, p. 921.

[45] Clark H. Pinnock, General Editor, *The Grace of God, the Will of Man* (Grand Rapids: Zondervan Publishing House, 1989). The book cover has as its first line the following: "A Case for Arminianism."

[46] The Grace of God, the Will of Man, p. 19.

[47] Ibid., p. 21.

[48] Ibid., p. 23.

[49] Ibid.

[50] Ibid., p.24

[51] Ibid., p.25. Of course, Calvinists affirm God's actions in history. The difference is that Calvinists see God's providence as the out-working of God's eternal decrees, rather than an experiential activity where God is responding to changing events in the world.

[52] Ibid. What becomes a possibility, of course, is that God might "mis-predict" something in a prophetic manner, resulting in God becoming a liar.

[53] R.C. Sproul, Chosen by God (Wheaton, Illinois: Tyndale House Publishers, 1986), pp. 25-26.

[54] Richard Rice, God's Foreknowledge and Man's Free Will (Minneapolis: Bethany House Publishers, 1985). Rice also has an article in *The Grace of God, the Will of Man* on "Divine Foreknowledge and Free-Will Theism." It is interesting to note, with reference to the purity of the gospel itself, that Rice is a Seventh-day Adventist. Anyone familiar with the Adventist doctrine of the "investigative judgment," which clearly identifies Adventist theology as "Galatian" in the sense of the necessity of human works for salvation, should see the danger of the alliance that is created by opposition to the doctrines of grace. The reader is also directed to the comments made by Dr. Robert Morey regarding both Rice and Pinnock. Robert Morey,

Battle of the Gods (Southbridge, Massachusetts: Crowne Publications, Inc., 1989), pp. 108-112 and 114-117.

[55] *God's Foreknowledge and Man's Free Will*, p. 33.

[56] Ibid., p. 39.

[57] Morey, *The Battle of the Gods*, p. 112.

[58] *God's Foreknowledge and Man's Free Will*, pp. 42-43.

[59] Ibid.

[60] Charles Hartshorne, *The Divine Relativity* (New Haven: Yale University Press, 1948) as cited in Hodgson and King, *Readings in Christian Theology* (Philadelphia: FortressPress, 1985), pp. 72-78.

[61] Hodgson and King, *Readings in Christian Theology* (Philadelphia: FortressPress, 1985), p. 77

[62] Ibid., pp. 136-141.

[63] Ibid., p. 137.

[64] Ibid.

[65] Ibid., p. 138.

[66] Ibid., pp. 138-139.

[67] Ibid.

[68] Remember Rice's words, "An open view of reality requires an open conception of God's relation to the world." It is not our views of reality that determine the truth about God or His relation to the world; God defines these things in His word, and we are to be conformed to that revelation. Rice, and fellow Arminians and process theologians have it backwards!

[69] *yozer*, Qal active participle, lit. "forming."

[70] *bore*, Qal active participle, lit. "creating."

[71] John Owen, The Death of Death in the Death of Christ, p. 78.

Scripture Index

196

The Mission Statement of Reformation Press

The ministry of Reformation Press was established to glorify The Lord Jesus Christ and to be used of Him to expand and edify the kingdom of God until Christ's glorious return. Reformation Press will seek to accomplish this mission by means of the publication of literature which is biblically faithful, and both relevant and practically applicable to many of the serious spiritual needs of mankind upon the verge of a new millennium. To do so we will seek to boldly incorporate the truths of Scripture which were largely articulated as a theology during the Protestant Reformation of the sixteenth century and ensuing years. We gladly join in the proclamations of—

Scripture Alone, Faith Alone, Grace Alone, Christ Alone, and God's Glory Alone!

Our ministry seeks the blessing of our God as we seek His face to both confirm and support our labors for Him. Our prayers for this work can be summarized by two verses from the Book of Psalms:

"And let the beauty of the LORD our God be upon us, And establish the work of our hands for us; Yes, establish the work of our hands." —Psalm 90:17

"Not unto us, O LORD, not unto us, but to your name give glory." —Psalm 115:1

Reformation Press appreciates monetary donations by anyone who shares our burden and vision for publishing literature combining sound Bible doctrine and practical exhortation in an age when so few so-called Christian publications do the same. All donations will be recognized by a receipt. Thank you in advance for any assistance you can give us in our labors to fulfill our mission.

Contact the publisher in
any of the following ways:

—write us at—
Reformation Press
160 37th Street
Lindenhurst, NY 11757

—call us at—
631. 956. 0998

—visit our website at—
www.reformationpress.com *or*
www.greatchristianbooks.com

—email us at—
reformationpress@email.com

Made in the USA
Coppell, TX
26 April 2023

16042755R10121